Born in 1904, **Syed Mujtaba Ali** was a prominent literary figure in Bengali literature. A polyglot, a scholar of Islamic studies and a traveller, Mujtaba Ali taught in Baroda and at Visva-Bharati University in Shantiniketan. *Deshe Bideshe* was his first published book (1948). By the time he died in 1974, he had more than two dozen books—fiction and non-fiction—to his credit.

A journalist for over three decades, **Nazes Afroz** has worked in both print and broadcasting in Kolkata and in London. He joined the BBC in London in 1998 and spent close to fifteen years with the organization. As a senior editor in the BBC, Nazes was in charge of South and Central Asia for a number of years. He has visited Afghanistan, Central Asia and West Asia regularly for over a decade. A passionate photographer and a compulsive traveller, Nazes quit his job in the BBC and moved back to India in 2013 where he is based in Delhi. He currently writes in English and Bengali for various newspapers and magazines and is working on a few photography projects.

TALES OF A
Voyager

(Joley Dangay)

Syed Mujtaba Ali

Translated by
NAZES AFROZ

SPEAKING TIGER BOOKS LLP
125A, Ground Floor, Shahpur Jat, near Asiad Village,
New Delhi 110049

First published by Speaking Tiger Books 2023

Copyright © Syed Mujtaba Ali 1955
Translation Copyright © Nazes Afroz 2023

ISBN: 978-93-5447-577-1
eISBN: 978-93-5447-584-9

10 9 8 7 6 5 4 3 2 1

All rights reserved.
No part of this publication may be reproduced, transmitted, or stored in
a retrieval system, in any form or by any means, electronic,
mechanical, photocopying, recording or otherwise,
without the prior permission of the publisher.

This book is sold subject to the condition that it shall not, by way of
trade or otherwise, be lent, resold, hired out, or otherwise
circulated, without the publisher's prior consent, in any
form of binding or cover other than
that in which it is published.

Translator's Introduction

What will you call someone who puts down his profession as 'quitting job regularly' while applying for his passport? The short answer is Syed Mujtaba Ali. Even though written in jest, this succinct phrase describes him perfectly—his wicked sense of humour, his peripatetic life, his ability of making fun of himself, his propensity of not settling down in one place or a job—everything can be packed into that phrase. And when these traits are gifted with a razor-sharp brain that masters a dozen languages and absorbs tomes on philosophy, history and knowledge from the four corners of the world, you get a Syed Mujtaba Ali. Only a few such unique persons are born in a century.

It was not a coincidence that a born rebel and non-conformist young Ali would be attracted to the greatest writer and philosopher of his time, Rabindranath Tagore. Refusing to go to a university run by the British rulers, he chose Visva-Bharati in Shantiniketan, founded by Tagore. Under Tagore's tutelage, the cocoon flourished into a dazzling butterfly. The teachings of Shantiniketan set the life course for Ali as Tagore remained his pole star.

Imbibing his guru's deep-seated ideals of freethinking humanism and internationalism, Ali as a twenty-three-year-old fresh graduate, would set out to explore the world. Starting as a teacher in Kabul in 1927, he went on to completing his PhD in comparative religion as a Humboldt scholar from Bonn, Germany, in 1932. After returning home briefly, Ali went to do his postdoctoral studies at one of the oldest universities in the world, Al-Azhar in Cairo in 1934. The ruler of Baroda state, Maharaja Sayaji Rao was hugely impressed by this young scholar when he met Ali during his visit to Cairo in 1935. The Maharaja invited him to head the government college in Baroda. Accepting the post, Ali moved to Baroda in 1936 and remained there till 1944.

Following the death of Sayaji Rao, Ali left Baroda and returned to Kolkata. He did not take up any jobs for a few years, concentrating on finishing his first book, *Deshe Bideshe*,* his memoir of his time in Kabul between 1927 and 1929. Serialized in 1948 in *Desh*, the most-read literary magazine in Kolkata, it was published as a

---

* Translated in English as *In a Land Far from Home/A Bengali in Afghanistan* by Nazes Afroz and published by Speaking Tiger (2015).

book in 1949. The book attained an instant cult status and Bengali readers were swept off their feet by Ali's prose, wit, gripping storytelling, ability to create a cast of most fascinating characters, and his multilingual and multicultural erudition.

Ali went through another life-altering event around this time. In the wake of the partition of Bengal, Ali moved to East Pakistan, which was his birthplace and joined the government college in Bogura in 1949 as the principal. But his stay in Pakistan was rather a short one. This was the time when Pakistani rulers were trying to impose Urdu as the national language over the majority Bengali population in East Pakistan. It was impossible for a freethinker like Ali who took a huge pride in his Bengali heritage and identity to subscribe to such a policy. He penned a short yet scathing critique of the government's attempt to colonize the Bengalis with another language. Pakistani authorities promptly issued an arrest warrant against him after the essay came out in a journal in Kolkata. Ali's elder brother, who happened to be a district administrator at the time, warned him about his impending arrest and overnight he left Pakistan forever. He returned to Kolkata and lived in India as an Indian citizen for the rest of his life.

Shortly after returning to India, the first Education Minister of India, Maulana Abul Kalam Azad, invited Ali to head the newly founded Indian Council for Cultural

Relations or the ICCR* as its first Secretary and the editor of its Arabic journal, *Thaqafat-ul-Hind*. He took up the assignment in 1950 before joining the All India Radio in Delhi in 1952. He went on to be the Station Director of All India Radio in Cuttack and Patna. Finally, he joined his alma mater, Visva-Bharati in Shantiniketan in 1958 first as a professor of the German language and then of Islamic Culture. After his retirement in 1964, as a full-time writer he lived between Shantiniketan and Kolkata.

As a man who led such an unorthodox life, his family life could not be otherwise. He married, late in his life (1951, at the age of forty-six), Rabeya Khatun, who worked for the education department in East Pakistan. They had two sons, born in 1952 and 1953. While he continued living in India as an Indian, his wife and sons lived in East Pakistan. After the freedom struggle and the war of independence of 1971 when East Pakistan became an independent country as Bangladesh, Ali started spending more time with his family in Bangladesh. He died in Dhaka in 1974 during one of such visits and was interred there.

***

---

* The ICCR was the brainchild of India's first Education Minister, Maulana Abul Kalam Azad, and was formed as part of the Education Ministry in 1950 to encourage India's cultural exchange with the world. Later it was made into a wing of the External Affairs Ministry.

Joley Dangay, literally meaning 'On Water and on Land', is Mujtaba Ali's only proper travelogue. Ali made several trips to Europe from 1929 to the early 1970s. His stories from these trips are strewn in many of his shorter pieces but he never wrote them as travelogues. They were stories of his friends, connections, various characters he came across and observations during the visits. So, they were not travel writings per se. This is his only book that fits the definition of a travelogue where he is describing his journey as it progresses.

In any travelogue, descriptions of the places one sees and the people one encounters become the centrepiece of the book. But here Ali had embarked on a journey to Europe on an Italian ship that sailed from Madras and the voyage lasted only for a couple of weeks or less. There was no opportunity for him to describe the places and people except for a brief stopover in the port of Djibouti. So, what does he do? He focuses on a few of his fellow passengers, and the history and society of the lands the ship passed like the Maldives, African coasts and Socotra Island. Like a master weaver, he spins a most attractive tapestry with a plethora of colours of little-known histories and unknown stories like the bringing of a giraffe from Africa to Bengal and then onto China, the perils of sailing past Socotra, how the kings from the coasts of Gujarat and Arab rulers from across the Arabian Sea came together to fight the Portuguese pirates or how the Somalis, led by Mullah Muhammad Bin Abdullah, defeated the Europeans in the

Horn of Africa. Readers get enriched as they go through every chapter of the book.

A reader might be curious to find out in which year he undertook the boat journey. From the book it is not clear when he made the voyage. There is no such reference in the text. The book was published in early 1955 (1363 in the Bengali calendar). So, the journey must have happened before that. In the text he laments how Indians are yet to get self-rule. Hence, one can safely conclude that he made the voyage before India became independent. But the Second World War would not have permitted him to go on a ship to Europe between 1939 and 1946. Even if he made the trip soon after the War, there would have been references to that catastrophic event. During his trips to Europe in the 1950s and 1960s, he constantly referred to the War and his observations about the changes that happened in the countries he had lived in before. So that leaves one small window—sometime between 1935 and 1939. Most likely he travelled a little before Europe was engulfed in the conflagration of the War.

My tryst with Mujtaba Ali occurred exactly five decades ago when I was in my early teens and was confined to bed, ailing from chicken pox. In my sickbed I could only lay my hands on two books by an author whose name was not known to me. Those were *Panchatantra*[*] and *Chacha*

---

[*] Published in 1952; Bengal Publishers, Kolkata.

Kahini,* collections of short stories and non-fiction pieces by Ali. They had such an impact on my young mind that his books became my lifetime companions.

Ali possessed the unique ability to offer a cast of characters who mesmerized his readers. He always presented them in such a way that it created the impression that he had actually met them. But having read all his books several times, I always suspected some of these characters were just a projection of his own self—erudite, well travelled, philosophical, deep, empathetic and affable. They possibly were a concoction of himself and some amount of imagination. His novel *Shabnam*,† a heart-wrenching tragic love story of a young couple—a Bengali scholar and a free-spirited Kabuli woman—set in Kabul when he lived there, is a testament of that suspicion.

Similarly, one such character takes the centre stage in this book too—Abul Asfia Noor Uddin Muhammad Abdul Karim Siddiqi! Abul Asfia, as Ali shortens his name later in the text, hardly talks but offers toffees, chocolates and cigarettes to fellow passengers from the depth of the pockets of his oversized coat. He also leads a plan of an overnight quick visit to Cairo after getting off at Port Suez and then again boarding the ship from Port Said on the other end of the Suez Canal. This service was offered by

---

* Published in 1952; New Age Publishers, Kolkata.
† Published in 1960; Triveni Publishers, Kolkata.

Cook, the ship's company, but was way too expensive for many passengers. Abul Asfia's plan attracted quite a few, including Ali and his two young friends, Paul and Percy. Despite having a lot of doubts, a dozen who did not have deep pockets like the first-class passengers, took the plunge with Asfia as they did not want to let go of the chance to see the pyramids. That short overnight journey becomes another entertaining adventure in the end. A discerning reader of Ali's books would end up wondering if Abul Asfia really existed or was it Ali himself!

Ali was a gastronome; thus, it is difficult to imagine his writings without elaborate descriptions of food, from street food to cafés to high-end restaurants and hotels. As an avid young reader of Ali, I was introduced to the concepts of so many cuisines—of course, without actually tasting them, but the ideas were ingrained in my memory and imagination. So later in my life when I had the opportunity to travel the world, I was always referring to Ali's texts while looking for a specific food in a particular land. One such description is there at a restaurant in Cairo in this book too:

> Peeking at the next table, I saw one man was about to start eating two cucumbers on a plate. How could two cucumbers, whatever the size might be, be enough for someone's dinner?...
>
> Who could tell what the food was?
>
> At that point I saw, instead of chewing the

cucumber, the man just pressed it in the middle and some pulau-like substance mixed with a few things oozed out. I was surprised to no end. I told the restaurant owner that whatever be my luck, I ought to eat those cucumbers.

Two cucumbers were served. After pressing them a little with a fork, the pulau came out. The pulau was mixed with small pieces of meat (what we call keema), slices of tomato and grated country cheese. I realized that all the stuffing had been put inside the boiled cucumber and finally it was fried in ghee. The same principle as our *dolma* of fish and *potol*—the only difference was here they had stuffed the cucumber with pulau, meat, tomato and cheese. Thus this was a truly superlative creation.

Decades after I read about this dish in *Joley Dangay* for the first time, I was in Cairo. A close Egyptian artist friend took me to a restaurant after a tour of the old market of Khan-el-Khalili. As we entered, in a flash my memory took me to Ali's description of the food that he tasted in the middle of the night. I asked my friend if we could get that stuffed-cucumber dish. He was curious and asked where I had found out about it. I told him about Ali and how he experienced the dish. My friend gave me its name—*kousa mahshi* or stuffed zucchini, not cucumber. He also told me that restaurants normally did not make that preparation but I should have told him before as his wife had prepared it that day. I was a bit sad for missing the chance of eating that dish but was at least happy to know the name. I was not aware that a surprise was in store. The following day my friend took me to his home and his wife was waiting with at least two dozen *kousa mahshi* for me!

Syed Mujtaba Ali opened up the windows to the world for a teenager and taught him, through his writings, how immersing in the world opens up one's eyes and broadens one's mind. He still continues to guide him in so many ways.

NAZES AFROZ
New Delhi, May 2023

1

The mission of undocking a ship from the quay is always a matter of pandemonium, a chaotic task. Two things that everyone gets to observe are: a lot of running around and shouting.

Some of you may think that white people perform all their tasks within a cloak of silence, while we cannot do anything without a hue and cry and making life unbearable for our neighbours. This sort of idea is not entirely wrong. You must have seen in films how the English eat at their banquets without making a sound. The butlers come and go silently; there's a muffled tinkling sound of forks and knives; people talk in low voices; everything is too well organized, well managed.

And what happens at our invitations, at our festival feasts, at our big gatherings?

Do I have the ability to describe that? Especially when my guru Sukumar Ray* has left behind this description in his unforgettable words. Listen to this:

---

* Bengali writer of nonsense and a well-known humorist.

> Come over, this way, with your dishes full of food,
> Stand and watch, it's a very very chaotic mood—
> Someone's calling for curd; another wants bread,
> Some are holding empty plates and crying instead.
> Over there, two Lords, with plates in their hands,
> Are squabbling as wildly as they possibly can.
> They all think they've power; for others they don't care—
> They're dying of hunger in this crazy affair!

What was he saying? Dying of hunger at a feast? Of course. Or how else could it be a Bengali invitation? If you do not like it, you are free to go to Firpo's. You can eat bland, half-cooked pig's head or the tail of some other animal.

But much like the howling sounds of all jackals sound the same, the noise when a ship undocks is the same anywhere in the world.

I have seen ships setting sail in Venice—the sailors on board and at the port, both on water and on land are macaroni-consuming Italians; I have seen the same in Marseille—sailors of both sides were authentic frog-eating French; I have observed it with full concentration in Dover—the monkeys at both ends were beef-steak-devouring raccoon-faced English. And there is no count how many times I have seen this contest on the Ganges, at Goalondo, Chandpur and Narayangunj.* On both sides they were my protégées—beard-waving, lungi-clad *Noakhalya* or *Sylhetya*.

---

* Ports in East Bengal, now in Bangladesh.

The shouts, the uproars, the hullabaloo in all ports are the same. Same smell, same taste. If you close your eyes, you will not be able to tell if you're listening to Chittagonian in Narayangunj or German in Hamburg.

Standing by the railing on the deck, you may be tempted into thinking that the sailors, both on the ship and on land, should have an agreement to get the ship released from the shackles of the ropes tying it to land. But brother, you will have made a great mistake. Actually the intention of both sides is to start some sort of a war. Unshackling or docking a ship is just a pretext. What the sailor, running from one end of the ship to the other is saying, by making faces at the sailor on land, cannot be heard in the din of the chaos but if you apply some imagination and if you have some knowledge of sailor psychology, you can understand that his simple statement is, 'You brainless idiot, can't you see that the rope is tangled on the left side? Do I have to put a mast in your eyes to show this? You'—(again swear words)—

Do not think that the sailor on land cannot give a fitting prompt reply either. You cannot hear his voice; you can only see his wonderful expression or rather contorting face and you have to imagine the rest.

He will noisily spit after looking up at the ship and say, 'You great primate, wrap your side properly. The pull of the ship will untangle the rope on my side. You don't know how a rope works and you've come to work on a ship? Won't you be better off going back to your village and picking nits in your granny's hair? You flat-faced'—(again swear words)—

Armed with the soap of imagination, you can thus blow many bubbles.

On the other side the ship's horn is blowing 'toot toot' over this ruckus—in Michael Madhusudan's[*] language, 'The tumult of chariot wheels—the clamour of great bows'.

It means, if it is a small boat, 'You lad, move aside. Can't you see that I'm on my way? You'll break into thirty-two pieces if I just brush against you. Will you put yourself back together by gluing yourself with the extract from marigold leaves?' If it is bigger than your ship, then it would mean, 'Greetings, big brother. Would you mind moving a little to your left so I can slip away from the right?' The sound of the horn also has a third meaning. If someone was getting drunk in the delight-juice, he will wake up instantly with the sound of the horn and run for his life to catch the ship.

Once I had seen a sailor swim to get to his ship. I had to close my ears and move away after hearing the swear words the other sailors hurled at him. There is an adage in English, 'He can swear like a sailor.' If you can avoid their language, you will become famous all over the world for being a sweet-talker.

---

[*] Michael Madhusudan Dutta, the writer and poet. This line is from 'Meghnad Badh Kabya'.

If you have a friend who has read Farsi, you can ask him the whole story of *Iskandar-e-roomira purshid*—meaning 'What Alexander the Great was asked'. The story was like this: Sikandar Shah was asked, 'Where did you learn to be so well behaved?' He replied, 'From ill-behaved people.' 'How is that possible?' 'I avoid what they do.'

I am not saying that it is a very witty story. But you will benefit if you can avoid the language of sailors, especially the English sailors.

At the dock you can also see a couple of people running up the gangway of the ship as it was being lifted. Why could they not come a little early? It is not like that. Someone was detained by Customs and he could only get through in the last minute; or someone on the wait-list got the news that another passenger had cancelled his trip and he got his berth; or someone got lost after going on shore to see the city and found his way just in time.

The ship was released from the port by saying, 'Badar, badar.'*

We want to sail the unknown seas, but our heart gets filled with an unspoken pain as we take leave of the shore. You may have all the feelings of freedom while looking around the vast expanse of the sea; you may have all the unparalleled experience of survival going through huge

---

* Guardian of the waters according to the Bengali Muslim belief, but revered by Hindu sailors and boatmen as well.

storms and big waves; but there is no comparison to the sweet feelings of coming back to the lap of the land. Hence, the guru of all travellers, Gurudev,* had said, after crossing many rivers, seas and oceans:

> 'Go back, go back to the shore's luring
>   The shore that's looking up spreading its wing.'

By the time the ship sailed, it had become dark. Leaning on the rails of the ship's astern, I stared at the megapolis, one of the biggest ports in the world, decorated with garlands of lights. There were streams of lamps in the streets, in the ships, in the fishing boats, or sometimes a lone one here and there, or a cluster as if it were a bunch of flowers.

We celebrate Diwali once a year, on an auspicious day. Here they have Diwali all year long. There's the auspicious moment every dusk. Their festival is all-inclusive; men and women from all faiths, all creeds—Hindu, Buddhist, Sikh, Jain, Parsi, Muslim, Christian—all take part in it.

I know that scientists say that some small birds are green in order to camouflage themselves in the leaves of the trees so that predatory birds cannot locate and swoop in on them. Like that, unripe mangoes are green too so that birds cannot see them. They become red when they ripen and birds then can snap them off the trees and the stone inside it will grow into another tree.

---

* Poet Rabindranath Tagore.

How can I say that the explanation of the scientists is wrong? How much of science do I know and what do I understand? But my simple beauty-seeking soul says, 'No, the bird is green because it looks beautiful in that colour and pleases my eyes. Be it big or small, there is no self-interest in it. It is green simply for the sake of beauty.'

Exactly like that I know that there are reasons for which each port gets flooded with evening lights. People get to see each other in those lights; a father can return home seeing those lights; a mother can find her child and get her household chores done. Still, when I see those lights from a distance, I tend to think that they are lit to make Diwali, the festival of lights, look glorious. There are no other reasons for it.

In the vast expanse of the sea, the lost sailor finds his way by looking at the stars. Yet Rabindranath has sung, ignoring that reason:

> 'You've lit the sky with so many lights
> For the festival.'

Looking at the lights of the port, I said to God:

> "We've lit so many lamps at your feet
> At the moment of homage."

Would that be saying too much?

We had now come far. The lights on the shore were fading. I saw a small fishing boat go past us in the opposite direction. But it did not go by. It was stationary there with its aft towards the sea and we simply passed it.

Was it not strange that they were catching fish so far from the shores this late at night?

What would they do if a storm picked up? If the boat sank, they would not be able to swim to the shore. Yet, why did they risk their lives by straying far into the sea? To make some money? Certainly not. I knew it rather well. I had lived for a few months at a friend's house on the coast in Madras. There was a fishermen's hamlet next to it. For six full months I had observed their lives. I was stunned to see their poverty. Poor peasants of our land were richer compared to them. Even our tribal people—Santhals, Bhils—lived more comfortably than them. Those of you who had seen the fishermen in Puri would agree with me.

Did they take so much risk and lead a life stricken with poverty because they could not find another occupation? My friend from Madras said that they so loved to live in the open expanse of the sea that they refused to till the land. During the stormy seasons they would go hungry, as they would not be able to go out in the sea to catch fish. They would venture out, ignoring the storm and die in the deep sea when they could no longer tolerate the cries of the starving children. Yet they would not leave the waters to look for a job on land.

And so it was also true for the boatmen and sailors. Their lives were not that cursed yet that they refused to go back to the land. Even a peasant, whose previous seven hundred generations had tilled the land, was forced to take up a sailing job during the famine and could not be persuaded to go back to farming. There was nothing more to say about the seasoned sailors. Their beard and hair become white; their skin turns bronze by the weathering of briny seawater and the salty air; there is no surety of how long they will live; no ship will give them any jobs anymore; yet they will stay in the congested alleys of Khidirpur[*] and run around from one liner to another searching for a job. They could easily go back home to spend their last days in the company of their grandchildren, sitting under the tamarind tree.

They have an 'addiction' to the sea and they are slightly coy about it. I do not know why it is so. If you said to them, 'So, Chowdhury's son'—they feel overjoyed if you address them as 'Chowdhury's son'—'you have saved quite a bit. Why do you have to take the trouble of working in liners any longer? Isn't it better for you to go back home and take God's and the Prophet's names thinking about the afterlife?'

He will say with a sad face, 'No sir, it's not like this.' He would then scratch his beard and say, 'It will be all right if I work for two more years. Without having some savings, it doesn't look good to become a burden on your grandchildren.'

Utter rubbish. The old man had taken up his job in a

---

[*] Port area of Kolkata.

ship when he was eighteen. He would be seventy now. For fifty-two years he had sent home money to build a proper house and acquire properties. Members of his family were now so well off that they could easily lend money to the landlord. And the old man was saying that his son-nephew-grandchildren would not give him two meals!

A few captains loved the sea so much that they built their house next to the sea in their old age. The shape of the house would be outlandish too. It did not look like a house but rather like a ship—to the best extent it could be on land. He kept stashed, in his penthouse room, a compass, binoculars, maps, steering wheels and other tools to run a ship. The old man would not allow anyone to enter that room because in a ship no one was allowed there without the proper uniform. Sitting there, he would bite his pipe and scold his 'seamen'. All the better if there were a storm. He would then be the superman—stomping around the 'bridge' to save the 'ship'; he would instruct the 'engine room' via the 'telephone' by shouting 'faster', 'full speed ahead'; and at times he put on his mackintosh and went out on the 'deck' to supervise and came back fully drenched. He would not have a moment's relief, let alone go to bed to sleep, until the storm died down. After the storm passed, he would say, 'Gosh, we had a close shave. All would have died sinking if I weren't here. The lads these days don't know how to steer a ship.' And then he would sit at the table to squiggle notes, thanking the crew of the 'ship' for saving it by executing his orders properly. After that he would take the bearing of the 'ship' by calculating latitude and longitude as it had strayed from its original course due to the storm. Finally, he might go down on his knees to thank God and go to bed, yawning, in his 'cabin' as a content man.

After three days, he will plod down from his 'ship' to the local public house to chat—as his 'ship' had just docked in the port. After giving a full hair-raising description of the killer storm, he will say, biting his pipe, 'No, it's enough. This is my last voyage. These old bones can't take such storms any longer.' Everyone will jump in showing sympathy, 'What's this, captain? This is no age at all.' The captain will come back happily to his 'ship' with smiles.

I know two more types of people who refuse to settle down.

I have seen gypsies in many countries. They will be here today and then there tomorrow. Day after tomorrow, they will be far, in another place. Which fair will start and close when and where—they know it all. They will visit those fairs to buy merchandise, dance and sing, tell your fortune by reading palms, but they will not stay in one place for long. They move in the blazing heat of the summer or during the non-stop rains of the monsoon. Who knows what attracts them. They have no urge to send children to school; they will not care to call the doctor if their children fall ill. Come what may, they will never build homes. They do not know the charm of home and will never find it.

In England they have been trying to settle these people for two hundred years. They were offered money, but they would never ever become the slave of one place. It is because of these gypsies that England has not been able to attain hundred per cent literacy. Finally the British have started travelling schools for them. Meaning the teachers are chasing them with pencil and board, but all is a waste; they are exactly what they are.

They are the children of unbound nature—they do not want to be get cloistered inside certain limits.

But do you know who far exceed them?

Rabindranath has written about them:

'I wish I were an Arab Bedouin
The vast desert under my feet fades into the horizon.'

We were heading towards the Aden port and crossing the Arabian Sea. They were the people of that land. From the dawns of Creation, they had been roaming the deserts of the Arab land. While moving about, they came close to the fertile green valleys of Iran or they had heard the songs of the leafy forests of Lebanon but they were never attracted to settle down in these places. On the contrary, the harsh reality of caravans perishing for want of water while crossing the desert from one oasis to another was not unknown to them, yet they walked those roads. The idea of settling permanently in one place is akin to getting struck by lightning for them.

I knew that the Arab land was very poor once. As it did not have the required resources, it could not set up artificial irrigation. As a result, they could never have agriculture. But recently the king of Najd-Hejaz* Ibn Saud made so many hundreds of millions of dollars by selling oil to the Americans that he did not know what to do with it. Finally, by buying modern equipment, he lifted groundwater to create farmlands and offered them to the Bedouins, saying they should quit the extreme nomadic lifestyle and settle in those lands.

But who listened!

Weeds the length of palm trees had grown on those lands.

The Bedouin was still roving here and there with his camels, mules, donkeys and horses. He was still spending the nights under the tent made of camel hide. Facing acute thirst, he would cut open the throat of his dear camel to drink water saved inside it. Finally he, along with his wife, children and animals may perish from thirst.

Yet he would not grow roots and settle somewhere.

***

I was immersed in such high thoughts. Meanwhile another fishing boat zipped past us. I saw that the old man had

---

* Saudi Arabia.

started cooking, lighting his iron stove inside his canvas shade. I could not tell if it was my imagination but I surely smelled *phoron*.* Imagination or not, my musing with theories stopped and I felt hungry instantly.

The last batch of dinner was long over.

It was nice to watch the surroundings and ruminate about various theories but it would be utterly foolish to ignore the pangs of hunger.

I thought of giving it a try once, or else I would go to bed by slapping my belly.

I hardly went ten steps when I saw my newly acquired young friends, Paul and Percy, were playing rummy. They got up in tandem and chorused, 'Good evening, sir.'

I said, 'Hello.'

I added with a tinge of complaint, 'You are playing cards without me? Don't you know that playing cards is a bad habit and is an unnecessary waste of time? Wise men have said...'

I had to shut up, as they did not try to stop me.

Percy said, 'Precisely so, sir.'

Paul said, 'So right. But we were busy getting dinner for you in your cabin...'

I said, 'What are you saying, boys?'

Percy said, 'Yes sir. We organized it when we saw that you didn't get up after hearing the dinner bell.'

---

* Indian spice condiments to add flavour to cooking.

Such first-rate lads. I wished to grab them under my wings and do a Naga dance. They might have been younger to me but by body mass they were no lightweights. So the desire to dance did not fly. I said, 'Let's go to the cabin then.'

2

Why do people go with the flow like sheep? The advantage in it is this: the consequence will be the same as for others. And because others in this life are living happily, you will also live like them with happiness and sorrow.

If you do not want to be part of the flock and want to walk the road alone, you may even find hidden treasures but then you may also turn the corner and see the mighty tiger is sitting in front, stretching his paws and swashing his tail.

And when you discover the hidden treasure all by yourself, it will be all yours but similarly, you would have to face the tiger alone.

Hence most people move with the flock, forsaking a hefty profit, fearing too much risk.

It was the same on the ship. If you got up with the rest, you might not get your morning cup of 'bed tea'. If you woke up too early or too late, you could get it instantly. But some days you might see that the oven was not even ready and hence the tea would be late. Or you woke up so late that the time for 'bed tea' was over and they had started breakfast. So you would lose your tea in the vast sea.

Hence it is said in English, 'No risk, no gain.' Meaning, there would be no profit if you were not ready to take some amount of risk. If you wanted to win the lottery, you at least needed to risk buying a ticket.

The risk did not pay off that morning. I sat on the deck with a long face after missing the morning tea.

Paul and Percy appeared in one minute.

Paul whispered in my ear, 'Have you seen the new birdies, sir?'

These were the new passengers, who had boarded the ship from Colombo. The poor souls were moving about looking to find a good spot to put their deck chairs. But where would they find such a place? We had already claimed possession of all places much earlier, from Madras.

This always happens. People go in a bit early to meetings or to a football match to lay claim to a good spot. I always sat just outside the kitchen door so my mother would serve food to me first.

There were two reasons to feel happy when one occupied a fine spot. The first was that you found a nice place and the second was even better. After taking a comfy seat, you could eat peanuts and look around dispassionately at others who were still in search of a good spot. Your glee would be beyond compare if you saw someone you knew and disliked him. 'Hello, Mr Bhar, are you looking for a place?' Then with a mischievous smile you could offer some free advice, 'There are so many places that side.' Waving your hands, you could then point aimlessly. Nobody would be able to understand where were the empty seats. Giving you a poisonous look, he would disappear from your vision grudgingly.

God had been kind enough to give us so many amusements. Who said that this life was an impermanent illusion? He possibly did not get a good seat at a football stadium.

I asked Paul and Percy, 'What's the plan for today, boys?'

Paul said, 'First, going to the gymnasium.'

'What's the schedule there?'

'Will row a little.'

'Rowing? Do they have boats and oars and water there?'

'Everything is there except water.'

'?'

'The oars are fixed with springs in such a way that it will give you the same resistance as if it is in water. So you could have the dry practice and the exercise of rowing.'

I said, 'Nope. Not attractive for me. In our land we row holding the paddle with both hands. Your ways of rowing will not suit me.'

Paul said, 'Then the parallel bars or dumbbells—something like that?'

'Nope.'

Percy said, 'Then Paul and I will box. You'll be the referee.'

'I don't know that theory.'

'We'll teach you.'

'Nope.'

Paul then said slowly, 'Actually, you don't want to get up and move. Let's forget exercising, everyone takes a stroll around the ship each morning and evening to keep their body fit. You don't even do that. Tell me why.'

I said, 'Will explain some other day. What else is happening today?'

Percy suggested, 'There is chamber music in the lounge at eleven. We could listen to that.'

Paul disagreed, 'The man who plays the violin creates such sounds, as if two tomcats are fighting.'

Percy said, 'This is Paul's problem. He's too finicky. You are going in a cheap French ship *Messagery Maritom* and you expect that Kreisler will come by your window to play his violin in the moonlight.'

I said, 'In our land an old woman went to the grocer to buy cooking oil for one penny. After returning home she saw there was a dead fly in it. She went back to the shop to complain and return the oil. The grocer said, "Did you expect an elephant in that oil worth one penny?"'

'Now I've got you, sir! I know a better English version of the story you've just told.'

Closing my eyes, I said to Percy, 'Narrate.'

'One old English woman, as finicky as Paul, had gone to the shop to buy a pair of socks. She wasn't happy with anything. Finally she bought the cheapest pair for one shilling. When the shopkeeper was packing the socks, she noticed a small ladder in one of them.'

I asked, 'What's a ladder? A ladder has steps.'

'If one of the threads in the sock comes out, then the cross threads create an impression that they are the rungs of a step. Hence it's called a ladder.'

'Thank you. Learned something new.'

'The woman said, "I won't take this pair. It has a ladder in it." The shopkeeper quipped, "Did you expect a marble staircase in a one-shilling sock, madam?"'

I said, 'Bravo. The story narrated by you can be considered a royal version of my story of daily chores. Besides, you're from the nation of kings.'

Percy said, 'Please sir, better not raise it.'

I closed my eyes, 'What has the ship company arranged to distract us from the monotony of the daily routines of the voyage?'

Percy said, 'As Paul doesn't want to listen to music, I'm thinking of getting a haircut.'

I said noisily, 'Never do that, Percy, even if they put a knife at your throat. They will cut your hair fine but at the same time the barber will shave you clean.'

'Didn't get that, sir.'

'It's a figure of speech in Urdu. They will cut your hair all right but at the same time they will shave your head.'

Percy was still in deep waters. He asked, 'If they cut my hair, then how will my head be shaved?'

I said, 'They will cut your hair literally but will shave your head metaphorically. The crux is they will rob you clean. Cutting hair will cost you five quid.'

'What are you saying, sir? In China you can have your hair cut twenty times for five pounds.'

'It's the same in India too. You don't pay five pounds to cut your hair even in the fashion capital of the world, Paris. It's like this: Rich people are going in first class. They don't pay less than that to have their hair cut. So the company has fixed the rate at five pounds. Forget us, even if a deck passenger goes to the barber, he'll have to pay the same rate.'

'Then what's the way out? What will our aunt think, when I land in London with a head full of wild hair? Besides, I'm going to meet her for the first time. Above all, the way my parents talk about our aunt, no doubt she's a formidable lady. Then I'd have throw five quid in the sea—literally.'

I said, 'Never. You'll have your hair cut in Djibouti. I have a feeling it'll not even cost you a shilling to have your hair cut there.'

Paul said, 'And we'll make a round of the port when Percy sits at the shack of the barber. He'll get a good lesson.'

Percy looked at me with sad eyes.

I said, 'Not like that. After doing the rounds, Percy will get his hair cut while we'll sit at the café to drink coffee. We may even sit outside the barber's to give him company and pass on some valuable knowledge.'

Paul stood up from his chair and said with a bow, 'What would we have done if we hadn't met you on this journey—'

I stopped him, 'Nothing would have happened. You would have gone around without having to listen to my gibberish and met younger people. You would have seen more and listened little.'

The duo vanished instantly.

I picked up a fat book about the weather patterns of the Arabian Sea.

3

No one should doubt that Bengalis are far more timid than Arabs. But in spite of being a sea and not a bay, the Arabian Sea is far quieter than the Bay of Bengal. Many passengers were down with seasickness between Madras and Colombo but they were up on their feet again once we entered the Arabian Sea. A gentle Nor'easter or *mousum* was blowing. Vasco da Gama had reached India using this wind in his sails. But that this wind blew towards India was not da Gama's discovery. The Arabs were aware of this wind, and as it used to blow during a certain season, they had termed it *mousum* or season. The English word 'monsoon' and the Bengali word *marshoom* were derived from *mousum*. Even after discovering the *mousum* wind, da Gama did not dare cross the Arabian Sea. He had brought along an Arab by force as his 'pilot'.

Romans were also somewhat aware of this wind. Or else how could they have conducted trade with southern India even before the Arabs? One still finds old Roman coins in many parts of southern India.

My limits of knowledge did not extend to how much the Greeks or the Phoenicians knew about this wind. I would be most glad if one of you could research this information and inform me.

Our ship was progressing by traversing this wind. There were no worries as long as the wind was gentle. The ship swayed a little and as it was blowing from the opposite direction, one would not get baked in this heat. But the whole ship prayed for a respite if it took the most violent shape. The book on weather patterns in the Arabian Sea had given the 'good news' a few times that at this time of the year the wind picked up twice or thrice a month to scatter the ships on the sea.

The meteorological sciences could forecast a storm but it would be impossible to predict in advance in which way the storm forming in the middle of the Arabian Sea would veer.

It was a danger for India if it moved east; as it would create havoc in Bombay, Karwar, Thiruvananthapuram (Sri Anantapur or Trivandrum). It would be a threat to the Persian Gulf and the Arabian coast if it steered north; the port of Aden and the Somaliland in Africa would face its wrath if it went west.

After one such storm, only one house in Obok, a town in Somaliland, survived. One could somewhat guess what such a storm, that ripped apart all houses on land, could do to a ship in the middle of the sea.

My firm belief was that a man will not face such a storm more than once in his lifetime. He would certainly reach the bottom of the sea at the very first assignation!

Was it right to say 'reaching the bottom of the sea'? I had read somewhere that ships did not reach the ocean bottom after they sank. At a certain depth, water becomes so heavy that the sunken ships are not able to penetrate it to go down any further. They then float in a limbo at that depth.

It felt strange to think that at a certain depth, all sunken ships are floating around until they disintegrate.

What happens in the waters possibly happens in the air too. If one floats balloons, they go up to a certain altitude and then hang there. They cannot go up or come down. Possibly with this knowledge, our ancient sages had imagined the state of *trishanku* or the 'limbo' between Heaven and the earth.

I would, of course, not be hanging in a limbo in any situation. The amount of food I was consuming all day long made sure that I would reach the bottom of the sea straight like a heavy rock. The weight I gained after each meal would easily penetrate the heavy waters. My only worry was with my head. It was so empty, as it did not contain any brain matter, that there was no surety when it would not dislodge from my torso and fly towards the heavens. If you ever want to recognize me in the middle of a crowd, you should look for the person who is holding his head with both his hands.

I noticed that my friend and my 'fellow pilgrim'—as we were headed for the same destination, no one should object if I called him my 'fellow pilgrim'—Paul had got hold of a telescope and was trying hard to spot something at a distance for some time. I first thought there was a ship passing by and that he was trying to read its name.

Seeing me stand up, he came close and said, 'Possibly land can be seen at a distance.'

I said, 'Not the mainland, but islands. Most likely it's one of the islands of the Maldives archipelago.'

Paul said, 'Never heard that name before.'

'How could you? There are so many people on board this ship. Ask them how many have been to the Maldives. Just ask if they have ever met a person from there. No one in this world has any interest in the Maldives.'

'How did you know?'

'I've heard that people of the Maldives are deeply religious. One man from there wanted his son to learn Islamic Studies. As there was no such facility in the Maldives, he sent his son to Al-Azhar University in Cairo—the best one to read Islamic Studies. I met the boy there. As we met many times, he filled me in about his country; but it was a long time ago and hence I don't remember a lot.

'There are about two thousand small islands and in most of them there are no inhabitants due to the lack of drinking water. The boy from the Maldives told me, "If you want to claim that on some ten or twenty of those islands you're the king, nobody will have any objection." There isn't much farming in the rest. The biggest island is just two miles long. The Sultan of the Maldives lives there and he has a small motorcar. But only he knows what pleasure he derives by driving on that two-mile-long road.

'The islands are full of coconut trees and the waters around the Maldives are crawling with various kinds of fish. They set sail with the *mousum* towards Sri Lanka with boats full of coconut and dried fish. The wind blows towards Sri Lanka at that season. They sell their merchandise all through the monsoon and in return they buy rice, pulses, clothes and kerosene oil. Even after finishing their trading, they apparently need to stay there for a while as the reverse wind doesn't pick up until the winter. So there is no way of coming back.'

Paul said, 'But why, sir, it's not winter. We're now travelling in the opposite direction of the wind.'

I said, 'Brother, our ship runs with the aid of an engine and not wind. Such mechanized boats don't go to the Maldives, as it doesn't pay. Hence no tourist has visited the Maldives ever.

'The lad from the Maldives had told me that, "There's no word for guest in our language. The reason is that no foreigner has visited us for hundreds of years. All our travels are very short as these islands are so close to each other. Hence we don't have to spend nights away from home." Then he had said, "You have an open invitation to visit the Maldives, but I know that you won't come. However, if you ever come by accident, you'll have to spend at least three years there. You'll eat and drink; you'll listen to music in the moonlight sitting under the coconut tree. What else do you need?"

'I can't deny that I wasn't tempted by that invitation. I wouldn't have to do anything for three whole years (the boy had also said that three and ninety-three were the same in the Maldives). Not only for three years, but I wouldn't have to do anything for the rest of my life. I feel that a light zephyr is blowing over the woodlands of my mind creating music just by imagining. I'll be rid of all pressures of examinations, all my little debts to every Tom, Dick and Harry and be free instantly. Oh what bliss!'

> 'What delight, what delight, what delight
> Freedom and shackles rave day and night—
> Tra la tam tam tra la tam tam tra la tam tam.'

It was not as if I divulged all these deep thoughts to Paul and Percy. But when they became excited with the prospect of spending all their lives in the Maldives, I remember telling them, 'Leave alone all your lives, you won't be able to spend even three months there. Because where there's nothing to do, your biggest job will be not to work. And it's the toughest of all jobs. Take for example, any other work like examinations—even that has an ending—BA,

MA, PhD—there're no more examinations after that. Say climbing mountains. There is a limit to that too—be it five, ten or thirty thousand feet. But the idea of "no work" is something that has no beginning and neither any ending. One can't handle things that have no endings.

'Or you can look at it from a different perspective.

'Our poet Rabindranath said, let's consider a room. The most important element of a room is its empty space inside—we can keep our furniture there, we eat and drink in it, by staying inside we save our bodies from the sun and rain. So most important is the empty space and not the solid walls. But you can't do away with the walls. Without the walls you get an open field where you can't get any shelter.

'Hence Gurudev has said, man's life is like the empty space of the room. It offers us the entry into a space but if you don't surround the empty space with walls of work, then it's of no use. And keep work to the minimum because you see that the empty space of the room is bigger in volume than the walls.'

Then I told them, 'But brethren, my guru has expressed this theory in a most gorgeous language mixed with some sweet and fun-filled Worcester sauce of metaphors. How can I imitate it?

'But the conclusion is this—the empty space of no work in the Maldives will become unbearable because it won't have the thinnest wall of work to surround it.'

I was so tired after talking for such a long time that I deposited my body on the deck chair.

I then noticed that Paul was scratching his neck again and again. Following that, he punched his head with his right fist and said, 'Got it, got it, I've now got it.'

Even before I asked what he got, Percy said, 'This is Paul's nature. He will scratch his neck repeatedly when he tries to remember something and he will hit his head with his fist as it comes to him. He does the same in classes and we make fun of him for that. Now let's hear what he has to say.'

Paul said, 'Nothing new, sir. The comparison given by your guru reminded me of a similar one that our guru Kung Fu-tsu or Confucius (I was really pleased to hear that this English young man showed respect by referring to Kung Fu-tsu as 'our guru', no English old or young man ever said that Buddha was 'our guru') had once given—if you allow me—'

I said, 'What pain! I'm done with your Chinese courtesy and decorum. Which monkey will not want to listen to Kung Fu-tsu's thoughts? Do you know that sage Kung Fu-tsu was a contemporary of our great thinker Buddha? At the same time Zoroaster or Zarathustra in Iran came to this world; Socrates-Plato-Aristotle in Greece; among the Jews in Palestine—but let it be. Now tell me what you were going to say.'

Paul said, 'Sorry, sorry. Kung Fu-tsu once said, "What's

the important element of a tea cup—its empty space or its porcelain body? We pour water, drinks, tea in the empty space. But without the porcelain the empty space would be of no use. So you need to surround your empty space of leisure time with the porcelain of work. And the thinner the porcelain, the more precious the cup is. So you should do at least some amount of work.'

Then he suddenly stood up and kow-towed, meaning he saluted me by bowing his head to his knee in the Chinese style and said—

I stopped him by saying, 'Again your Chinese courtesy?'

He replied, 'Sorry, sorry. But sir, today the inner meaning of Kung Fu-tsu became clear to me as we discussed the stories of the Maldives and your guru's thoughts. I've heard his teachings and read his sermons many times, but it's only today that—'

'Plug your mouth,' I said.

4

In some ships, they cooled the air by some chemical means and circulated it in all its sections. It was as if a mother was caressing the sun-baked ship with high fever with her cold hands to give it some respite. But for how long? At least a train got the chance to rest under the refuge of trees when it stopped at stations; or it got the cover of the shadows of the mountains when it ran through a valley; or while running through the *sal* woods it got the affectionate shade of the forest. And it would be best if it ran through a tunnel—it would feel like the inside of an icebox. But a ship had no such luck. On the one hand, the sunrays were lighting cremation pyres all around until the horizon; on the other, the sun was magnifying its power by reflecting on the waters. One could not look at it even when wearing dark glasses. There was some light cool breeze at night but before one could chill a bit, the sun-teacher would be up again with his whips of rays. God had given him millions of hands and with those hands he had taken up millions of golden bamboo canes. Seeing that, one's body hairs would stand in fear.

Our ship had no such system of circulating cold air—meaning it was not air-conditioned. So be it night or day, no one could get any chance to sleep properly on the Bay of Bengal, the Arabian Sea and the Red Sea.

The breeze might pick up from midnight. You sat in the deck to cool yourself. But there was no way you could go inside the cabin to catch some sleep. That cool breeze could not enter the cabins; so it would be unbearably hot inside. It was like going to the *maidan*[*] to cool yourself before coming back to sleep in the stuffy house inside the alleyway.

You could not get some sleep on the deck either. Say, you closed your eyes at two in the morning. The crew would flood the decks with buckets of water at four o'clock in such a way that even a fish could not sleep there. Where would you go then? If you went back to the cabin, you would feel that it was the bread oven—you would be roasted in there.

This would go on until one reached the Mediterranean.

But the only consolation was that young people were not bothered by the cold or the heat like us. So when Paul and Percy snored inside their cabin, I used to sit out on the deck looking at the stars. At that time I did not feel like reading a book or writing letters to family and friends back home.

---

[*] The empty open ground in central Kolkata.

Sometimes I fell asleep on the deck chair.

One night, I suddenly woke up and saw a strange figure in front of me.

The gentleman was wearing coat-trousers-tie all right but his trousers were slacker than pyjamas, his coat had reached his knees and the tie could be vaguely seen penetrating his flowing solid beard. Looking at his dress and other trappings—I was mistaken, I did not notice his trappings at first sight, I saw them gradually later. Right then, I saw that apart from two breast pockets, his coat had a couple of extra pockets. Possibly it had come down to his knees because of that.

I had not seen him on the ship earlier. Where had he been hiding? Had he then boarded the ship from Colombo? Where was he for the last two days?

The gentleman blurted, 'Good night.'

I was not abreast with Western etiquettes that well but I knew this much that 'good night' in that culture was an address to take leave. It was like our ways—when we say 'let me come'. So at a first meeting if someone said, 'let me come', one understood that he was not a Bengali. So I guessed from his 'good night' that he might be attired in the Western style but he was in fact an Indian.

I said, '*Baithiye*—please sit.'

To my left was Percy's empty chair. He sat on it and said, 'My name is Abul Asfia Noor Uddin Muhammad Abdul Karim Siddiqi.'

I involuntarily said, 'Gosh.' Would I have to explain why? Still let me say.

I am a Muslim. My name is Syed Mujtaba Ali. My father's name was Syed Sikander Ali and my grandfather's name was Syed Musharraf Ali. Normally Indian Muslims have triple-barrelled names. So was it surprising that I was taken aback hearing his name of two and half yards' length?

I guessed he too knew this. Taking a seat, he took out a magnificent gold case from one of his main pockets. He took out a visiting card from there and said, 'My name is a bit too long. So keep this.'

I was even more awed. I was aware of cases in which visiting cards are kept, as they were generally beautiful and slim. People like insurance agents, newspaper journalists or canvassers of votes, who carried such cards, normally used them. But they used cases made of German silver. I had not seen a gold case for cards before.

Even before I got over the awe, his hand dived deep inside one of the pockets and brought out a gold cigarette case. I had seen such cases in dreams and in the hands of film stars in the cinema. It was the first time that I saw a similar case in reality. It glittered in the low lights of the deck in such a way that it could only be compared with newly made jewellery. On one corner of the case, two or three initials of his name were studded with some kind of blue stone. The case was large as well. It could easily hold thirty cigarettes. He held out the case to me and from another pocket he took out a lighter. It was decorated with Jaipur-style *meena* etching. At first sight it looked like an amulet of the first lady of a rich landlord family.

Like an army of soldiers, at least fifty questions paraded through my mind.

The most important of all was, why did he keep so many beautiful expensive items in the pockets of such a worn-out coat and trousers?

The second one was, why was the person who possessed such expensive objects travelling in tourist class with poor people like us instead of using first class?

The third question was—we would rather do without it. A whole day would pass if I had to give a list of all my questions about him. You too are intelligent and hence I am sure the same questions would come to your mind after hearing the description of the gentleman. Then why should I elaborate on those?

But how to get answers to these questions?

He was lot older than me. How could I start questioning him if he did not start the conversation? Our elders' order was, as I had been hearing from my childhood, seniors asked and juniors answered. How could I disobey such a diktat? Especially in a foreign land where I did not know the local etiquette. Was there any way other than following what the elders had taught?

Half an hour had passed. I finished burning two cigarettes. I had to say 'no' firmly when he offered the third stick. At the same time, I asked after gathering some courage, 'Where are you going?'

He looked as if he did not hear the question. I too did not press him.

After a while I said, 'If you will excuse me, I'm going to retire now. Good night.' He said, 'Good night.'

Who could tell why he did not talk. It might be that he had rheumatism in his tongue. Or it might be that there was a rationing on conversation in his country. Whatever it was, there was no point thinking more about this.

In the morning, when I was busy discussing and solving all of life's difficult questions with Paul and Percy, the gentleman appeared again. As soon as I introduced them to him, he took out a handful of Swiss chocolates, English toffees and American chewing gums. Paul and Percy took a few, but he would not withdraw his hand, despite them saying, 'No, no, it's enough.' Again, he had not a single word to say. Finally, with a sad face he sat down on a chair.

After feigning a little, we got back to our conversation. Then we realized that he did not like to talk but he had a full appetite for listening. He kept saying, 'yes', 'right' at the appropriate places. Eventually he got up after failing to offer us lime squash.

Soon after he left, I asked Paul, 'What sort of birdie is he?'

Paul said, 'He boarded the ship from Colombo. His pockets were full of confectionary. He had been offering something or other to whomever he met. But I haven't heard him talk yet.'

I said, 'I need to ask him.'

Paul said, 'Will you get any reply?'

'Righto. I didn't get anything last night.'

The reason I have talked so much about him here is because we struck a deep friendship with him later. I will relate that story when the time comes.

5

Paul said in a wise tone, 'It's 2081 miles from Colombo to Aden port; takes six days. There are no islands on that stretch, at least on my map. But Socotra Island lies just before Aden. We may be able to see it.'

I said, 'How will you see if we pass that area at night? And even if we pass it during the day, I don't think we'll sail close to it. Because small islands hide under the waters close to big islands. If we were to ram into one of them, then we would go down rather than going forward.'

I kept talking but it felt that I had possibly heard the name Socotra somewhere. Suddenly a lightning flashed through my brain. My father's maternal aunt and her husband had gone to Mecca for Haj with their two sons towards the end of the last century and I had heard many stories from that trip. This grandaunt of mine was a master storyteller. She would keep us awake at night by telling stories while dinner was being cooked. As soon as my aunts gave the news that dinner was ready, she would wrap up her stories instantly. We never realized that the story she left us with was a monkey without a tail. We always thought it was a wingless fairy queen.

I heard from that grandaunt that the passengers used to feel at their worst when their ships approached the Socotra Island. Slapped by the currents of the waves and crazy winds, often ships would bump into the submerged islands and break into a thousand pieces. Some passengers clung onto the planks of the ship, some grabbed the moss-covered rocks and shouted, 'Save us! Save us!'. But who would save them? Where were the lights and where was the land? Slowly they lost their hold and disappeared into the bottom of the sea.

The way my grandaunt described it, I would forget everything and start wondering if my grandaunt survived or did she drown too. It never occurred to me that she was telling the story with me on her lap. Finally she used to say, 'It didn't happen to our ship. It was the other ship. Your friend Moina Mian's granddad was on it. You know that he never returned. God has taken him to Heaven. If someone dies on his way to Mecca to perform the Haj, he goes straight to Heaven without going through the trials of his sins and good deeds.'

She could tell the stories for a long time and repeat them many times. Every time it felt that I was hearing the old story in a new shape. Or you could say, this was akin to us seeing our new sister-in-law sometimes in a Rash-mondal sari and sometimes in Bulbul Chashm. (Alas, where have those beautiful saris gone!)

Thinking about my grandaunt's stories now, I feel that she possibly took help from the tales of the *Arabian Nights* in her descriptions. There are so many stories of sea voyages, shipwrecks, unknown lands and islands in the tales of the *Arabian Nights*. Reading the exploits of Sinbad the Sailor, it feels as if the custodian of waters, *Badar Pir*, had written a law by which Sinbad had to be on every ship that was ever wrecked.

The main reason for so many stories of sea voyages in the *Arabian Nights* was that the Arabs once ruled the seas, in the way one sees American and British ships in every port these days. It was not difficult to understand why it was so. The Arab land was surrounded by seas on all three sides. So they were not afraid of the sea the way we are not scared of the Padma–Meghna rivers, though Indians from the western provinces take the name of the monkey god Hanuman when they first see the Padma at Goalondo—possibly because the river is as expansive as the sea here. Before the Arabs, the rulers of the seas and oceans were the Romans. The Arabs defeated them gradually to have unfettered access to sea routes. One can see that Mecca is not far from the sea. After that, the Arabs took the help of the monsoon winds to cross the Red Sea and began trading with India.

While I was thinking of such connections, I suddenly remembered Socotra again. My grandaunt's stories reminded me that the Greeks had named Socotra as

'Dioscorides'. This in turn reminded me instantly that according to many scholars, the name 'Dioscorides' had originated from the Sanskrit word *'Dwip-sukhadhar'*. When the Arabs landed here for the first time they had a conflict with Indian pirates. It was difficult to ascertain for how long that conflict continued, but the heads of the Indian societies had, by then, started imposing an embargo on crossing the seas. Maybe without any help from India, the pirates either slowly disappeared or got integrated with the locals like the way India's millennia-old connections with Siam, Indochina or Indonesia snapped at some point.* Most likely it happened due to the embargo imposed on sea voyages. But the Indians had left a footprint on Socotra; the cows there were of the same breed as those of the Indus valley. It was really strange that humans disappeared in the conflicts of various civilizations but the traces of its domesticated animals like horses or cows lived on for centuries, reminding the curious ones of their original masters. The Mughal-Pathan era of India ended a long time ago, but can we say for how long the roses brought by them will continue to give us fragrance?

Whenever I closed my eyes and got lost in my thoughts, Paul and Percy would leave their chairs and get busy doing something or the other. I went round to look for them

---

* Reference to Indian Hindu society's ban on sea voyages introduced around the eighth century.

and saw that they were writing letters sitting in the lounge. Seeing me, Percy asked, 'Will this letter reach China with the French postage of the ship?'

I said, 'Certainly. Even if you post it at Djibouti, it'll go because the Djibouti port is under French rule. But if you post it from Port Said, the postage will be invalid in Egypt and the letter will go in bearing post.'

'But what if I post it in the ship's letterbox after reaching Port Said?'

'It'll be all right then.'

Then I said, 'That'll be fine but it'll be better if you get off at the port and send it with Egyptian postage.'

'Why, sir?'

I said, 'I do recall that you have a younger sister living in China. She surely collects stamps. What's the benefit if you use French postage at every port? Won't she be happy to get Egyptian stamps? That too, on her elder brother's letter?'

Percy started the same refrain—the same way when I solved his problem of the haircuts—'If he had not met me...'

By that time Paul had joined me. He asked softly, 'What were you thinking when we talked about Socotra?'

I said, 'A lot.' And I told him some of it.

I had seen that Paul was not a busybody like Percy who was always doing something or the other. He read books sitting in a corner of the ship at times. Now he silently digested what I said and then replied, 'The topic is really interesting. Who ruled the seas first, who after that and why did they too lose out, now that the Americans and the British are ruling the waves? But for how long? Who will prevail after this?'

After thinking a little I said, 'Possibly the black people of Africa. The Phoenicians, the Greeks, the Romans, the Indians, the Chinese, the Arabs, the Portuguese, the Dutch, all of them ruled one after another—only they were left out. Possibly it's their turn. Look at the map; it's a massive continent; it's buzzing with millions of healthy and strong men and women.'

Paul said, 'But education and intelligence?'

I said, 'It's a matter of two generations. Once started, a race can overtake another in hundred years. Rather, it's tough to rejuvenate an old, half-dead civilized race to put them on a pedestal. It's difficult to give a new shape to a figure that has already been moulded and that is the new problem of the Indian, Chinese and other ancient races.'

Paul asked, 'Did the Indians also rule the seas?'

I said, 'Almost everyone has forgotten that. But one shouldn't blame them. Even the Indians don't keep track of their own history. As far as I know, they traded from the Red Sea to the China Sea and ruled over Siam, Indochina and Indonesia. After that, one day our heads of society banned venturing out onto the sea. It's likely that they didn't like expanding our empire. So they possibly wanted to say, "Get integrated with the locals of the country you've won, no need to come back home."'

Paul said, 'I spent sixteen years of my life in China, but never heard that it had any contacts with India. Only thing I heard was that Buddhism had reached China from India. But that too is complex stuff.'

I said, 'Totally, don't try to tread that route. But there was a funny contact between India and China. Want to hear it?'

Paul said, 'That goes without saying. But where is Percy? He's always going round the way a puppy tries to catch his own tail. Oi Percy!'

The Giraffe's Tale

When the Mughals and the Pathans were ruling over Delhi, Bengal always tried to gain independence at the slightest opportunity. The main advantage that Bengal had was that it was waterlocked with so many rivers, canals, lakes and marshy areas. The Mughals and Pathans had never seen that in their motherland or even in Delhi. So they faced great difficulty when they came to Bengal to quell the rebellions. The land was slippery, and they could fall if they did not have the experience of treading that land.

At one such opportune moment, one ruler of Bengal became independent. The king was a bit whimsical. Why else would he send an emissary with many expensive gifts to faraway Iran to invite Iran's most famed poet Hafiz to

Bengal? In the invitation he wrote, 'Oh poet, the whole of Iran is now full with your melodious and sweet voice. Iran is a small country, it doesn't have enough space for your voice to flourish. On the other hand, India is a much bigger land—please come here, your voice will have plenty of space here.' The gist was, how many people in Iran would be able to appreciate him properly? This country has a much bigger population, so he should come here.

Hafiz was aged by then. His old bones were not ready to make such a long journey and live in a foreign land. So the poet wrote a long and beautiful poem explaining why he was declining the invitation.

Official documents in Bengal don't have any mention of this episode. This history can be traced from Iran's archives.[**]

Then the king's sight fell on China. But one could not invite the emperor of China to Bengal. So an emissary was dispatched to China with plenty of high-quality gifts and good wishes to the king.

The Chinese emperor was overjoyed after receiving the courteous gestures. China was a rich country. So he reciprocated by sending even more expensive gifts. But that king had by then gone to the land of the King of kings.

[**] At one time, Hafiz was widely read in Bengal. Even now one reads, 'No sights yet I wish to see your misty face, no ears yet I wish to hear buzzing bees' in the Bengali translation of *Sadbhab Shatak*. The best translation of Hafiz in Bengali has been done by Krishna Chandra Majumder.

The new king then thought about what he could give to the Chinese emperor that he did not have. He expressed his thoughts to the emissary and asked for his advice. The emissary was a wise man. While staying in China, he had inquired in detail about the lifestyle of its people, their beliefs and faiths. He said to the king, 'Many Chinese people believe that there is an animal taller than the trees and if ever that animal comes to China, then the crops of China will be as tall as this animal.'

The king asked, 'Which animal?'

The emissary said, 'The giraffe. One finds it only in Africa.'

The king commanded, 'Bring it from there.'

As if it was an easy job! Here was Bengal, so far from Africa. Would it be easy to put a giraffe on the great modern steamships that roamed the world these days? Who knew how many months or years it took for a sailing ship of those days to reach Bengal from Africa and then on to China? How would they get fodder for the animal in the sea or look after it properly? Even on this mechanical vessel, they served us small amounts of vegetable and salad.

Travelling via Africa, Socotra and Sinhala, the Arab traders used to trade with Bengal in those days. The king instructed, 'Bring me a giraffe.'

The giraffe arrived. I would not be able to tell what it ate on the way or how long it took for it to arrive. The king was satisfied seeing the giraffe. He ordered, 'Send this to the Chinese emperor as a gift.'

There was China. By ship. No one knew how many days it took to reach there.

One could only guess how elated the emperor was. He instructed that a high stable be built for the animal.

Who could say that its head will not touch the clouds or bump into the moon?

When the giraffe was rested enough after such a long journey, on one fine auspicious day and moment, the emperor, along with his ministers and court members, came in a procession to see the giraffe. He brought with him his court painter and the poet laureate.

The emperor was amply pleased seeing the giraffe. The court members exalted him repeatedly. The mass of people was greatly delighted—their forefathers did not lie when they had prophesied that such a wondrous animal existed on earth and it would come to the Chinese land one day. The neck of the sceptics, who never believed it, should be stretched like that of the giraffe.

The emperor asked the painter, 'You draw the most beautiful painting to commemorate the day for eternity.'

The painting was done.

The emperor told the poet, 'You put the descriptions of the auspicious day in verses along with the painting.'

So it was done.

After finishing the story, I said, 'I've seen the copy of the painting in a newspaper.'

Paul asked, 'Sir, do you know Chinese?'

I said, 'Not at all. One of my friends is learning Chinese in order to read Buddhist scriptures in that language. Possibly you know that many of our ancient scriptures were destroyed with the decline of Buddhism in India. But they are still available in Chinese translations. My friend came across this story while searching for Buddhist scriptures. He had it translated and published in Bengali with the copy of the painting in a newspaper. Or else Bengalis would never have known of this because there is no mention of it in our history books or documents in the archives in Bengal.'

Percy said, 'But sir, it didn't sound like history. It exceeds fiction.'

I replied, 'Why, brother? There is the saying in your language, "Truth is stranger than fiction."'

And my personal opinion was that if the narrative of an event could not rouse interest in someone more than fiction, then that event had no historical value. Or I would say that the narrator was not a true historian. In our land, most of our historians are such dry bores.

6

Noise, shouting, loud wailing. What exactly was happening? Had the ship been attacked by pirates? Was it like what we saw in the bioscopes and the pirates were attacking by jumping from one ship to another with two pistols in two hands and a dagger between their teeth? Suddenly there will be an ear-piercing all-destroying explosion—the gunpowder room will explode after catching fire. Then that fire will spread to the sails and ropes and finally consume the whole ship.

No. Dream. Relief. My whole body was wet with sweat. After opening my eyes, I saw all the lights in my cabin were on and Paul and Percy were standing before me. Paul was standing straight but Percy was doing some kind of strange Zulu or Hottentot African dance—it surely had to be an African dance as we were passing by the continent.

Be it an African Hottentot jig or the destructive dance of Lord Shiva—I could not even differentiate between the European Mazurka or Lambeth-walk dances, more so their music. But why had Percy started dancing in my cabin without any notice?

No, it was not a dance. He was jumping up and down in excitement and the summary of his wailing was something like:

'Alas sir, all is lost, everything is gone and you're still snoring? My life's ruined, Paul's life too. The ship has swum overnight and reached the Djibouti port. Everyone on the ship is ready to get off after finishing breakfast and you're still—what a pity, sir, what a pity!'

(If this book is ever made into a film, then there will be tears and repeated deep sighs at this point.)

Percy howled when I closed my eyes again.

I calmly asked, 'Why am I hearing the sound of the engine if the ship has already reached Djibouti?'

Containing his impatience Percy said, 'Switching off the engine is just a matter of minutes.'

I said, 'From the experience of my previous boat journeys, I know that it takes at least a couple of hours for the ship to dock after the engine is switched off.'

Paul opened his mouth for the first time, 'But we can see the port clearly.'

I said, 'You can see the peak of Kanchenjunga from Darjeeling. But can you reach it in ten minutes?'

Then I added, 'But that's a fallacious argument. I'm going to prove my point right now.'

I started shaving leisurely and slowly. Paul was assured after hearing me but Percy was still jumpy. In a bid to hurry me, he handed me the toothbrush instead of the shaving brush. It would have taken no time to turn my face into that of a langur if I used it to lather my face. He gave me the gown rope instead of my tie. Then he made a strange hodgepodge of tea-bread-butter-eggs to offer me and then started to circle around—like how the puppy of the house runs through everybody's legs annoyingly as they pack their luggage before travelling.

Under pressure, I too hastened a bit and we trooped on to the deck.

By that time, other passengers, getting fed up, had resigned to their games of cards, chequers and chitchat.

Training his binoculars, Paul said, 'Where is the port, sir? All I can see is the vast expanse of desert and a few rows of tin-roofed boring houses.'

'This is the port of Djibouti,' I said.

'What's there to see in this desert?'

'Nothing. But you shouldn't be that picky while travelling through a foreign land—especially at this age. When you've entered the zoo, you should see the raccoon along with the tigers and the lions. And who knows you won't have an incredible experience while turning an unknown corner? After reaching your destination you can take stock of things you liked and didn't like.'

One can walk down the stairs from the ship comfortably at all major ports in the world. But here we could get to the port on a motor launch. There may be worse ports in the world than Djibouti but it was so far the ugliest and most uninteresting port I had ever seen. It had been built at the corner of the desert with the sole aim of expanding empires. And knowing fully well that it was impossible to create greeneries around it, no one had ever tried to make the area comfortable.

A straight dusty road stretched to the *chawk* or the town centre from the port. A few streets and lanes went in different directions from there. But who would want to explore those after seeing the main road? The whitewashed houses on both sides of the main road stood with such depressing fronts that their inhabitants most likely halted for a few moments, scratched the right side of their neck with the left before entering them. Peeking into one of the lanes, I saw small mud-walled and mud-roofed houses. No, not houses; one could say caves or craters. It rained so little in this land that there was no possibility of water entering the rooms from the roof. Even if it did, the land did not produce any grass or foliage that could be used to thatch them.

People lived here regardless; mothers loved their children; brothers loved their brothers; birth-death-marriage—everything still took place here.

But why was I surprised? Did I not ever enter the congested slums of Kolkata? Did I not see the level of poverty and misfortune there? Then why was I getting so surprised here? It might be that I did not expect this in a foreign land or that I was so used to seeing our own poverty and misery that I was astonished to see it in a different form in another country.

Here was the difference between great men and ordinary people. Great men never get used to seeing poverty. They never say: it happens everywhere; it occurs daily; we have been seeing it from our childhood. Misery pains them deeply always—though often it is not apparent from their demeanour. Then they get an opportunity—the opportunity they were waiting for all their lives, or the opportunity they had been building on every day, every moment. Rabindranath has described this:

> Long have you shunned fame and glory O great-
> anchorite, as the mountain cataract
> Bursts forth from rocks with full force in monsoons,
> So have you risen; Bewildered, the wide world wondered
> with your mantle that
> Overshadowed the firmament; where were you
> shrouded, inconspicuous, for all these days!

So suddenly, when one Aurobindo Ghose,[*] or one Chittaranjan Das,[†] appeared in our midst, our surprise held no limits. People like them who were born with silver

---

[*] Bengali revolutionary who waged war against the British. After his arrest and time in prison, he turned spiritual and founded the Aurobindo Ashram in Pondicherry.

[†] Bengali barrister and freedom fighter. Was a leader of the Congress party in Bengal and the first Mayor of the Kolkata Corporation. Broke away from the Congress party to form the Swaraj Party in 1923.

spoons in their mouth and grew up in lavish affluence all their lives, could give up everything one day and go out to help the poor, have-nots, unfortunate and the unwanted mass. They underwent great pains in their attempts to eradicate the misery that had pained them so much. But the truth had to prevail in the end.

> —Do we hear
> His triumphal conch? So, in your able hands
> With affection firm, He now entrusts
> The flaming torch of misery; Its glow
> Pierces the darkness of this nation.
> Like the Polaris. Victory to you!

But why am I narrating all this to you? Because sitting on the ship, I was thinking all night about the African continent and Somaliland in which the Djibouti port was located. I was repeatedly remembering the man who gave his life fighting foreign enemies in order to assuage the misery of the Somalis.

To read the history of the African continent is to apprise oneself of the naked face of European barbarism. The history of colonial India ruled by Britain is nothing in comparison.

The Portuguese, the English, the Germans, the French, the Belgians—what more should I say? Every European nation, big or small, once pounced on Africa with the monstrous appetite of expanding empires in the way a flock of vultures attacks a cow. A mistake: I was being unfair to vultures, as they would never attack a live animal. These Europeans flocked around the Somalis, the Bantus and the Hottentots. After shackling and packing them like caged chickens, they took them to America in shiploads. One has read descriptions in books like *Uncle Tom's Cabin* of how tens of thousands of the African people died facing incredibly painful torture. I read it in translation when I was young.

The history of what they did in Africa has yet to be written. Famous French author André Gide drew a lot of flak after writing about this. Only someone as courageous as him could think of writing such a book. But even if one wrote a book, who would publish it? Even if they got a publisher, they would face severe attacks in papers; and there would be vulgar reviews. Then sellers would refuse to keep the book in their bookshops. But it is good to know that there are still some people who write such books, publish them, sell them and that people read them. That is how people have protested against injustice; that is how movements take shape.

Many nations came to rule over the Somali people. Finally, only the French, the British and the Italians prevailed.

It was Mullah Muhammad Bin Abdullah who first started the fight in British Somaliland in 1899. With unrelenting courage, unarmed or armed, only with broken old guns and bows and arrows, the Somalis gathered around him to face the European cannons and machine guns. The British and the Italians were fighting over the control of Somaliland, but they conveniently patched up to crush Muhammad's attempts of gaining independence.

Both sides won and lost many battles but finally the Mullah chased the British down to the shores of the Red Sea. Giving up hope of ruling over the Somalis, the British stationed themselves by building a fort on the sea to save the Red Sea ports.

The whole of Somaliland hollered: 'Somalis are independent.' Then the British named him the 'Mad Mullah' the way they named our Gandhi the 'Naked Fakir'. Was it not true that one could only make faces after losing badly?

But not many years have passed since. The Europeans have learned the tricks of conquering people by bombing them from aeroplanes. When they attacked the Mullah with their new arsenal, he had no other option but to accept defeat for the time being and take shelter in another country.

In the face of daunting challenges, the Mullah again set off to make new plans to achieve independence. But alas, following twenty-two years of war and going through rigorous struggles, his health had started failing. A year after his last defeat, taking the name of the God in whose name he had started the independence struggle, he left for a realm where possibly there was no divide between blacks and whites.

The tall and robust Somalis had apparently broken down in wails after hearing the news of his death.

We draw inspiration by hearing stories of brave people. Or else why would I remember this sad story? But before that, I need to emphasize something.

It is meaningless to say, 'The French are bad people' or 'The English are a nation of thieves.' There are many pickpockets in India but it would be unjust to say, 'All Indians are pickpockets.' It also made no sense to say, 'The English are tyrants.'

We should not take up arms by giving up patience in the face of injustice or anarchy. Many nations have tried that but there was no lasting result. It just contributed to more violence and bloodshed.

Hence the Mahatma professed the message of non-violence. One needs to win over violence with non-violence. There is no other better teaching than this one. India will be considered the world's most civil country if it can pacify the world's conflicts, wars, looting and exploitations with this idea.

And the final words—the most important too—were—

We should never develop the greed to conquer other countries. We should learn from the unjust behaviour of others. For two hundred years, we lived under the rule of other people. We knew the pain of that subjugation. We should never subjugate any other nation.

7

Paul asked, 'Sir, what are you staring at so intently? I can see nothing that is soothing to the eye here.'

I replied, 'I'm trying to be Sherlock Holmes. Can you see that man walking down the road? He came out of that shop, right? The signboard says, "Friseur"; so looking at the hair on the back of his head, I am trying to figure out in which category the barbers of this land belong.'

Percy said, 'Yes, yes. Good that you remembered. I'd completely forgotten that I needed a haircut. Let's enter the shop.'

I quipped, 'You may but it seems they cut hair with scythes in this country.'

Percy said, 'Let them use a scythe or a sickle, I have no other option.'

The barber did not know any language other than French. I somehow explained Percy's need.

But the shop was so small that Paul and I did not get a place to sit inside. There was no veranda either. I told Percy to join us at the café located at the crossroad after he was done with his haircut.

There was only one café at the crossroad. As all its doors were open, we could see that it was crowded with customers. But this port was the size of the palm of one's hand; how come there was such a gathering, like that of a cattle fair?

After entering the café, we realized that it was as if we were back in our ship's dining room! Its customers were our very own co-passengers. It took them ten minutes to 'visit' this port, and so they were all in the only café of the land. Hence the café was chock-a-block. They found their own tables. The way they sat in groups of fours or sixes in the ship's dining room, they were seated in exactly the same way with their 'families' here too.

A few people were sitting pensively in the corner with a blank gaze. We had not seen them on the ship. I guessed they were inhabitants of Djibouti. Their attires were torn and crumpled.

But we will talk about all that later. What we noticed first after entering the place were the flies. I used the word 'notice' in its literal sense as a swarm of flies practically brushed my eyes.

The flies were spread on the café table, making patterns; they swarmed to the bar counter; on the backs or the hats of the customers—there was not a single place which they were afraid to invade.

As soon as two glasses of lemon squash were served to our table, at least eight flies took up their positions on the rims. When Paul tried to shoo them away with his hand, a few dropped in his glass of squash. Paul said, 'Oh no.'

I asked, 'Shall I order another glass?'

He said courteously, 'No, sir. As is it, I'm feeling queasy. There's no need to spend any more money.'

By then the waiter had handed over two flywhisks to us. We started to fan away the flies in chorus with the other customers.

It was a most bizarre scene. About fifty customers were waving their flywhisks all around, as though staking their lives for an invisible king. Flywhisks to the right, flywhisks to the left, flywhisks above and flywhisks below the table. Getting chased, the flies, whether in swarms or alone, were entering Paul's nostrils and, in some cases, my mouth. Conversations had stopped. There was a whoosh of flywhisks and the buzzing of flies all around. It was like a Russian–German battle.

Only the four original inhabitants of Djibouti sat there silently, unperturbed. I guessed that they were used to the flies as well as the passengers of ships fighting with flies. They had been seeing this commotion every day.

At that point I noticed their trick of drinking squash. They did not use the fan, neither did they try to chase the flies with their hands. Just before they took a sip, they tapped on the glass gently. With that the flies left the glass rim and hovered three inches above and they very quickly took their sip. They did not have any qualms.

It caught Paul's eyes too and he whispered in my ears. 'Why do these people live in this godforsaken place?'

I said, 'That's a rather long story. If you ask each of them, you'll learn many long and fascinating stories of their lives.'

In this world, there are people who would like to become millionaires overnight. They are not cut out to run farms or orchards, to do business or trade or to take up some kind of job. Who would want to slog so much? This is not their dispensation.

You people must have seen in films that with the rumours of finding gold somewhere in Africa where lumps of gold are supposedly scattered above and below the ground, hordes of fortune seekers go out to look for that gold in a bid to become rich overnight. Films exaggerate these journeys so much; people dying of thirst; dead bodies strewn all over. In some place, parents and children are moving in a broken van—the son is vomiting blood, the daughter is unconscious. The father is trudging along with a tin canister looking for water and getting injured while tripping over rocks. The mother has not a single drop of tear in her eyes—she is almost numb.

Moving along, moving along, they are moving along. There is no way out. They will face a sure death if they stop; they might just survive if they move forward.

There had not been any official or unofficial census of how many of them reached 'el Dorado', how many could get the gold, how many of them came back to their societies and enjoyed the riches they got. And what if there was a count? Could information from such a census stop those people who had such an addiction in their bones?

Sometimes one of them would float a company to raise funds by selling shares. Why? Some pirate captain apparently disappeared with treasures worth millions to some unknown island. The island needed to be located to find the hidden treasure. No passenger or cargo ship made any voyage in the sea in which the island was situated. Apparently there was no drinking water on the island. The pirate captain had possibly died of thirst. So many such rumours.

The man, who floated the company, spread the word that he had the map to go to the island. People said, 'Show us the map.' The man said, 'What cheek! What's the guarantee that you will not go and grab the treasures?' But people who wanted to become rich overnight normally did not ask many questions. They did not buy shares of the company even if they had money. They went to plead with the promoter, 'Take us on the ship as seaman, cook—in any capacity. We don't want any salary or wages.' The captain was looking for such people—strong, able-bodied men who were not afraid to die.

Then one day the ship set sail. But it never returned.

Then only a few men came back. As they could not find any treasure, they had killed the captain. The police was after them. There would be cases. And why not?

Looking at the four people from Djibouti, Paul asked in a hushed tone, 'Are they all such people?'

I said, 'No, but their descendants. By descendants, I don't want to mean these are the progenies of those people because such people don't normally settle down after marrying. By descendants, I mean these are people of the same category—ones who would like to become rich instantly. But these days the rumours of hidden treasures don't get the chance to spread much, as newspapers, after investigating by hiring planes, report that it's all bogus news. Or there is no need to hire a ship. One can do the survey quickly from a plane. It's become easier with the invention of helicopters. They can land on the spot to search properly.

'So these people are involved in opium smuggling. Or they run guns, machine guns and other weapons if there's a rebellion or civil war in some land. When their enterprises fail, or they use up all the money they had made, they come to a godforsaken port like Djibouti to earn a little and to dream of new impossible adventures as they're now old with little strength left. They somehow find work here. Take for example, the railroad that has started from here and gone up to Addis Ababa, the capital of Abyssinia—almost a five-hundred-mile stretch. There are so many odd jobs besides trading that happens along the way. They're involved in some such work and in their spare time they tell tales of the adventures of their younger days.'

In case Paul misunderstood, I clarified quickly, 'But I don't want to imply that those four people are such adventurers. It's a possibility—that's all.'

Meanwhile I started to cough as a fly entered my mouth. After I recovered, Paul asked, 'Hearing their life stories from you, I'm not sure whether I should pity them or have some other reaction.'

Thinking a little, I said, 'You know what I think? When one seeks pity, we need to ask the question if the person is pitiable or not. But these people don't care for anything or anyone. They keep their hopes alive until the end of their lives and dream that at the turn of a road or at the bend of the river, they will see the fantasy land where the trees have leaves made of silver, the fruits made of gold and with their touch the dews on the grass turn into diamonds, where—'

I had the longing to be more poetic but Percy, chasing flies, arrived at that point. Sitting at the table, he presented a large bottle of Eau de Cologne. Smile on the face and happiness in the eyes—not the bottle's but Percy's.

Taking it in my hand, I saw it was the most expensive Eau de Cologne—the water of Cologne made in the city of Cologne—the 4711 brand!

Percy said, 'Made a killing, sir! Tell me how much it will cost in Bombay or London?'

I said, 'Maybe twelve to fourteen shillings.'

The way Percy smiled, even Ramachandraji did not

have such a smile of satisfaction after winning over Lanka and rescuing Sita. But from Percy's chest thumping we could guess what Hanuman had done.

'Three shillings, sir, three shillings! Right now, in total, just three shillings! Not a penny more, not even a red farthing more.'

At that moment I saw that Abul Asfia—etc. etc.—Siddiqi, in his long coat and loose pantaloons was walking towards us. He was our generous friend who always treated us with lime juice and chocolate—but all his stinginess was in his talking.

We all stood up to receive him.

After taking a seat, he took the bottle in his hand and started scanning it from all sides like the way doctors look at X-ray plates.

Percy said with a smirk, 'Totally genuine stuff.'

Keeping his mouth closed, Abul Asfia said with his nose, 'Hmm.'

Then with a lot of unwillingness he moved his tongue and asked, 'For whom did you buy this?'

Percy said, 'For my aunt.'

Abul Asfia said, 'If you don't open the cap of the bottle, you will have to pay a lot of Customs duty while disembarking in London. Even while embarking the ship now—but I'm not so sure about that.'

Percy looked at me.

I said, 'If you open the seal of the bottle, it'll be treated as your own—for your own use; hence you don't have to pay any tax.'

Taking his time, Abul Asfia said, 'As you have to open it in the end, you can do it right now.'

We all—Percy too—agreed, 'That's best.'

The waiter brought a corkscrew. Using that, Abul Asfia opened the bottle neatly and smelled the bottom of the cork before taking a whiff of the stuff inside.

After thinking a little, he then made us smell it.

There was no aroma.

As if water—plain 'authentic' water.

Percy was dumbfounded. Gathering himself after a while, he said slowly, 'But the cap, the seal—all looked right, untouched.'

Abul Asfia said, 'In these small ports there isn't much oversight by police. So many people use various means to take out the real stuff and fill the bottles with water or adulterated liquid.'

I pulled Paul aside to whisper, 'Possibly one of the "adventurers".'

I observed that the Djibouti locals sitting at the next table were giving us sympathetic looks. It was not difficult to figure out that they had guessed what had actually happened.

Percy, by then, somewhat understood too. He said, 'The passengers are simpletons and hence this con can be pulled on them. And each ship is full of—'

Paul interjected, 'Percy.'

Percy retorted angrily, 'Ha! As if you're a Kung Fu-tsu.'

While boarding the ship, I found Abul Asfia alone and said, 'You really disappointed the lad.'

He replied, 'There wasn't any other way. Or else he would have been conned at every port.'

8

Wise people say that one should only make thoughtful and judicious comments.

While leaving Djibouti, Percy cursed, staring at the port, 'Godforsaken place.' He still had not got over the Eau de Cologne episode. So he said it without thinking much.

A storm picked up in about an hour or so. It was not a dangerous one but enough to knock people down with seasickness. Percy took to the bed first. His face had turned green by continuously throwing up. His cheeks had collapsed, making him look like a seventy-year-old man.

It was not as if I was feeling too well; still I said to Percy, 'So my dear son, you were cursing the Djibouti port a while ago. You'll be fine in two minutes if you can set your foot on that godforsaken land. You must never be dismissive of dry land—at least when one is away from her—be that on a ship or in a submarine or flying through the air on a plane. But let it be. Now you know why wise people say what they say about thoughtful comments?'

But Percy was a crafty chap. In the middle of his

tossing and turning he somehow yelped, 'But right now if the ship crashes on submerged land and sinks, will you still be praising the land?'

I said, 'Ah, ha! I didn't think that far ahead.'

Paul was listening to our conversation sitting on his bed. He slowly said, 'If the ship crashes on a piece of submerged land then it's not the fault of the land. The ship is going at speed; hence it breaks and sinks. It will come to a halt if it sails slowly. Why would it break? If you push your mother hard, she'll give a slap in return; so why won't the land?'

I said jubilantly, 'Bravo! The parallel you've drawn is superb. But the saddest part is that you won't understand the pun you've made with the two words we use in Bengali. One is *Ma* meaning mother and the other is *mati* meaning "the mother" or the "earth".'

Paul said, 'Understood it perfectly—Good Earth.'

Percy said annoyedly, 'Paul must have stolen the example from somewhere.'

I said, 'An honest man sells two seers* of milk for one rupee and a thief too takes a rupee for the same two seers of diluted milk. The value of money remains the same. Paul's example can be original or taken from somewhere but the parallel was good. But let it be. You won't die of seasickness. Nobody has ever died of this "sickness".'

---

* Old Indian unit of weight, which is slightly more than a kilogram.

Percy said feebly, 'You dashed my last hope, sir! I was hoping that I wouldn't have to suffer much and be relieved as I would die soon.'

Paul said, 'Parasites don't die easily.'

I said, 'Okay, okay. Paul, let's go upstairs to the deck. The three of us are giving too much importance to seasickness.'

While leaving the cabin, Paul quipped, 'Rightly said. The disease, left alone with Percy, will desperately look for a way to escape.'

Coming up, we saw Abul Asfia had managed to lay his hands on a pair of powerful binoculars and was intently trying to look at something on the horizon. These ships did not sail close to the shore. So it was not possible to see anything around. Paul asked me. 'What is he trying to see?'

I replied, 'Abul Asfia is a Muslim and it seems he's faithful to his religion. Somaliland, the land of the Habsis,* and Misr† are on one side of the Red Sea. On the other is Arabia. Prophet Muhammad was born in that country and preached Islam from there. Mecca and Medina are located in that land.'

Paul asked, 'When one wants to refer to a place to be the centre of something they mention it as "the Mecca". You must know that in the field of music, people say

---

* People of African origin.

† Egypt.

"Vienna is the Mecca of music". What is this reference of Mecca? Mecca isn't a big city anyway.'

I said, 'There are only three world religions—meaning the religions that are not confined to their countries of origin and have spread to faraway places. Take for example, Buddhism, Christianity and Islam. But unlike the way Muslims gather in Mecca for the Haj, the followers of Buddhism and Christianity don't get together in one particular place on a special auspicious day. How far are Morocco, Siberia or China? You'll find Muslims from every country where there's a presence of Islam in Mecca that day. I've heard that on that day you can hear almost every language on the earth in Mecca.'

'What's the benefit?'

I said, 'The people of Mecca certainly benefit from it as they get all the money that the pilgrims spend. But the custom wasn't set for that reason. Muhammad Sahib's wish was that if all the Muslims of the world could be gathered for one occasion, then their sense of fraternity and unity would increase. When we go to the mosque or the church for prayers instead of praying at home, the objective is to meet people of the same faith. Muhammad Sahib possibly wanted to do the same but on a much larger scale—with the whole world.'

After thinking a bit, Paul said, 'We don't get together at Lord Jesus' birthplace Bethlehem for Christmas. Wouldn't it have been better? That way the friendship and unity among Christians would have been better forged.'

I thought even more and replied, 'Then possibly the influence of the Roman Pope would have reduced.'

But let it rest here. I hope any Catholic reader of this book will not think that I have no respect for the Pope. As tens of million people of the world revere someone, I cannot be disrespectful to him. If I do, then I will be showing disrespect to those tens of million people. I have no such arrogance, particularly when I am Indian. We have been hearing from our childhood that we should respect every religion.

9

The storm was over. The sea was calm. As there was no breeze after the storm, it was unbearably hot and stuffy. What could we do to get respite from this pain?

People were doing what they would have done on land. A few were really intelligent. They immersed themselves in work so much that they became oblivious to the tyranny of the heat. The only sufferers were the fools who only did one thing at a time, and then fiddled with another thing the next. They tried to sleep, and then suffered more by waking up again.

The same happened on the ship. One group played cards day and night. After eating a breakfast of bread and eggs in the morning, they dived so deep into the card game that it would be impossible to drag them out until well past midnight. They left their cards once or twice for lunch and supper—that was all. At that time they either said, 'Oh, how hot it is'; or they discussed their card games at the meal table, 'It would have been better to call three no-trumps instead of four diamonds, and it was foolish not to have doubled that!'

Unofficial records in the archives of ships claimed that it was not rare to see people playing cards for thirty-six hours at a stretch. They do not suffer in the heat, nor do they succumb to the cold. God is kind to them.

The tradition of playing chess is in decline worldwide. In fact, chess players can beat anyone in this regard. Unless one sees it, one cannot believe how chess players can lose all senses when they play the game. Parashuram* had written that the servant came and told his master who was engrossed in playing chess, 'Sir, how can I make tea? The milk has split.' The man, absorbed in his game, replied, 'What a nuisance! Why don't you stitch it together?'

One group only read books. But most of them were reading detective novels. I rarely saw people reading worthwhile books all day long.

Another group was engaged in chitchat. Mixed with that, in a hushed tone—essential for any such repartee—there was gossiping and backbiting. I will not give out details as a reader might just ask, 'How did you know unless you were also involved in such gossiping?' Hence I will refrain from listing them.

There were other combinations, many other groups, but Abul Asfia did not belong to any of them. He sat with the group engaged in chin-wagging but he did not

---

* Pen name of Rajshekhar Basu—well-known Bengali writer, chemist and lexicographer from the late nineteenth and early twentieth century. He wrote his comic and satirical stories under the pen name of Parashuram.

chitchat—like the boatman of the ferry who rowed from one bank to the other with passengers but does not get off the boat. I have described it earlier but his appearance was different today. Let me explain.

After getting better, Percy was again running around the ship. Wherever I went, there was a Percy. Sometimes I wondered if Percy had eight twin brothers. Or else how could one man be present at seven places at the same time?

He brought the news.

What news?

The ship would enter the Suez Canal after reaching Suez Port. The Canal was a hundred miles long. As both of its banks were sandy, the ship could only progress at a speed of five miles an hour. So it would take twenty to twenty-two hours to cross the Canal. Suez Port was at one end of the Canal and Port Said at the other. If we got off at Port Suez, took a train to Cairo to see the pyramids and took the train again to Port Said, we would be able to board our ship. Even though we would traverse two sides of a triangle—the Suez Canal being the other—we would have about ten hours in Cairo to see the city, as we would be travelling much faster on the train.

But what if we did not get the train on time at Suez Port, or if we missed the right train to Port Said from Cairo and as a result we missed the ship?

Percy said impatiently, 'That's the responsibility of Cook Company. They're the ones who have organized this trip or excursion—whatever you call it. Every ship offers this trip. Many people go. Come with me to the noticeboard, I'll show you the notice.'

We, the three musketeers, went there and read the notice with full concentration.

But reading the last paragraph, our senses exploded with a bang and not a whimper. For people who wanted to take this excursion—a picnic or a city tour, whichever it was—would cost each person seven pounds or one hundred rupees. Paul said, 'Hari, Hari,' (in English it would be something like 'good heavens' or 'my goodness'). 'If I had so much money, I would be travelling in first class on this ship.'

Faking hurt sentiment, I said, 'Why, brother? Are we such bad people that you would've chosen first class to avoid us?'

Caught off guard, Paul became red in embarrassment and started stammering.

And Percy? Jumping like a langur, he started dancing and said, 'Serves you right, serves you right. Go ahead and make more jokes with sir. It'll serve you right.'

I said, 'Okay, okay. Enough, enough. But Percy, a hundred rupees is no joking matter. Finally, I will have to balance my budget.'

It was difficult to contain Percy. He said, 'Take no offence, sir. Do you think I'm a Henry Ford or King Midas or perhaps a Rothschild? I've decided I will certainly see the pyramids spending the last pennies in my pocket. After seeing the Great Wall of China, how can I not see the pyramids? How will I be able to show my face to others? Most importantly, how will I look at my own face in the mirror?'

We discussed it a great deal; we deliberated at length. Finally, it was concluded that our fate did not allow us to see the pyramids. With our hands on our cheeks, in the pose of a thinker, we were trying to get over the grief when Abul Asfia opened his mouth.

Keeping to his true tradition, he was listening to us. He did not make a single comment—good or bad. When we decided that we would not take the trip, he said, 'It can be done a lot cheaper.'

We shouted in unison, 'How? How?'

He said, 'Will discuss it later.'

Then he left his chair and walked towards the dining room.

10

I did not see much of Paul and Percy the following days. Like a postal stamp, they attached themselves to the coat of Abul Asfia. It would be an understatement if I said they were latched onto him like a leech, because leeches at least come off once they have sucked enough blood—but these two were going about with Abul Asfia much like the way a stamp moves along with the envelope. There was just one refrain on their lips, just one query—how can one go to Cairo on the cheap and then again what was the cheap option to go on to Port Said from there in time to catch the ship? Abul Asfia kept saying, 'All will be disclosed—at the right time.'

Finally, a day before the ship was to arrive at Suez Port, he unveiled the mystery. It was rather simple but we never thought of it.

Abul Asfia said, 'Cook Company will take passengers—the rich Europeans on first class—from Suez to Cairo and again from Cairo to Port Said. They'll also arrange an aristocratic hotel for their night stay, which will naturally be rather expensive. We will travel third class and will stay at a cheap hotel. That's all.'

We were surprised at first. Once I recovered my senses, the thought of a tough problem clouded my mind. If we were to miss a train at some point, or if we were to face an accident and finally, if we were unable to reach Port Said in time to board our ship, then we would be at our wit's end. There were solutions for when one was on the platform to have tea and the train left with one's luggage. But we did not know for how long we would be stranded at Port Said and how much it would cost us to stay there or how much extra we would have to spend for our new tickets. Those in charge at Cook Company would be responsible for all that but how could we pass such responsibilities on to Abul Asfia? We would not be able to tell him, 'Sir, we are having to spend extra because of you—you need to pay for us.'

When I expressed my worries omitting that last bit, he stood up and left. Before leaving he uttered only one sentence, 'No risk, no gain.' The crux was 'Tom drank wine and Harry is having a hangover—that doesn't happen.' If you decided to drink, you would have to deal with the hangover. If you wanted to catch the catfish, you will have to put your hand inside the hole. There is no gain of any sorts unless one is ready to take some amount of risk.

Paul said in a worried tone, 'That's true', after hearing those four words from Abul Asfia, 'No risk, no gain.'

I too said, 'Yes.'

Paul said, 'Let's assume we get lost in the streets of Cairo. Does Abul Asfia know the language of Cairo? I don't even know which language is spoken there.'

Percy responded, 'Listen, Paul, now is not the time of making a list of what you know and what you don't. It would take a rather long time to do that anyway.'

'Again!' I scolded Percy mockingly. I told Paul, 'Arabic. But there will be a few who would know English or French. We will surely find the way.'

Paul said, 'I'm sure we'll find our way. But possibly by then the ship will be gone, leaving us behind.'

We discussed many other potential troubles. Simply put, would it be wise to go to an unfamiliar land for such a trip without knowing the language and with such little time in hand? If it was this cheap and easy, then why were so many people taking the trip on the tail of Cook Company? They could easily have gone alone or in their little groups. So in effect the phrase of Abul Asfia, 'No risk, no gain', would, in our case, mean a gain of sixty per cent and a risk of eighty. Rabindranath had said,

> 'The world means well, in my opinion
> If bad is forty-three, good is fifty-seven.'

If the odds were indeed fifty-seven to forty-three in our favour, we may as well take a splash saying 'Ya Allah' as we would be going to a Muslim country.

Finally it was decided that we would not make up our mind without properly interrogating Abul Asfia once more.

After crawling here and there, after a lot of searching, we found Abul Asfia in the corner of the upper deck, humming a tune. Seeing us and before we said anything, he said in a raised tone, 'I don't want to hear anything. I can't give any more answers. I will go to Cairo. It will be good if you all come, and even better if you don't.'

Along with that, it seemed I heard a word, '*Bujh-dil*'—a Farsi word for 'Goat's liver', meaning 'All cowards'.

We did not expect such behaviour from a gentle soul and amiable person like him. It was like a commander's order, 'You may come or not, I'll be fighting the enemy soldiers all alone.' Beaten up, we, the three musketeers, came back to our seats with our tails between our hind legs like scared dogs. Nobody said a single word. We ate silently before retiring to our cabins.

The old adage of 'Don't stir the lion's tail' held much truth, but it was not clear in which category we could put Abul Asfia—a lion or langur. It was unclear whether his behaviour was gallant or simply vacuous.

11

After waking up next morning and going up to the deck, I witnessed a great hullabaloo and commotion around Abul Asfia. Surrounding him, a group of people was asking him many questions. 'Cook Company is charging hundred rupees for a trip to Cairo but you're saying it can be done for fifty?' Another group was saying that they too were keen to come but what would be the solution if in case they missed the ship?

So, it seemed, poorer passengers like us had found out that there was a cheaper way to visit Cairo and see the pyramids. It was no longer Paul, Percy and I—the three musketeers—and a quartet including Abul Asfia. The problem now was multifaceted; the people had risen.

Abul Asfia was repeating once in a while, '*Ho jayega, sab ho jayega,*'—'It'll be done. All will be arranged.'

Why was he talking Hindustani? He knew English well. Then I noticed that the crowd surrounding him included French, German, Spaniard, Russians and so many other nationalities. There was no single language that all of them would understand. So he was safely talking in his mother tongue. Speaking in English or in Hindustani would have the same effect.

At that point, the most beautiful woman in our midst, said in the sweetest and most compassionate voice, 'Monsieur Abul, we'll be in a soup if we somehow miss our ship. As you are not taking us forcibly, we will not be able to hold you responsible.'

The woman, most elegantly, laid out what was on the minds of all present there. Everyone chorused in their own languages to express themselves.

The French group: *Oui, oui.*

The Germans: *Ja, ja.*

The Italian team: *Si, si.*

The only Russian: *Da, da.*

Few Indians: *Thik hai, thik hai.*

Paul and Percy: Yes, yes.

I did not say anything—but let that be.

Keeping his head down, Abul Asfia said, '*Main jimmedar hoon*'—'I'll be responsible.'

He was taking full charge when no one had asked him to be accountable—it would be his responsibility.

12

A Bengali, looking for a job, reached the house of his potential employer—an Englishman—and said in a bid to butter him up, 'Sir, I was so scared to come to your house that I couldn't move forward. If I took a step ahead, I would go three steps back.' Not all bosses are stupid—this one had intelligence. As soon as the Babu finished, he asked, 'Then how did you reach my house?' The man did not expect that the Sahib would take his words of flattery so literally. He stumbled at first but a job-seeking Bengali has all the tricks up his sleeve and is not to be deterred. Without batting an eyelid, he replied, 'So sir, I turned my back to your house and now here I am.'

I did not remember the rest of the story but the people queuing up for Abul Asfia's Cairo trip were also going three steps back after each step forward. Except for Paul, Percy and me, there was not a single confirmed signatory. There were random questions every minute. What if we miss the train; what if we do not get hotel rooms in Cairo; how will we see the pyramids if there is no moon—such was the array of bizarre questions. Meanwhile, Abul Asfia was sleeping in his cabin after locking the door and we were having to face the barrage of questions as if we were the King of England, George the Fifth, or his Viceroy of India. Finally, we too started retreating from the battlefield.

The ship reached the Suez Canal just before evening. The steamer from the port came to dock with the ship soon after anchoring at the mouth of the Canal. We then found out that nine of us were going as a team with Abul Asfia—including him we were ten.

The guide of Cook Company came on board from the steamer. We saw twelve people were going with him. So our team of ten was no less strong.

The guide went down in the launch and the twelve followed him the way sinners crossed the Baitarani river,* holding the tails of cows or the Panda. Our Abul Asfia got off with an air of a seasoned guide.

The Cook guide had not seen any such scene before. It looked unbelievable to him that a group of people was going on their own—taking such risks—without his supervision and guidance. Had he been Durvasa,† Abul Asfia would have been turned into ashes from the looks he gave him. He was eating into his business.

---

* The river, in Hindu mythology, that one crosses after dying to reach the afterlife.

† The sage in Hindu mythology, who was known for his anger and ability to burn down people just by looking at them.

At that point, we looked properly at Abul Asfia's new clothes. He had taken off the loose long coat with eighteen pockets and the narrow pantaloons that touched the ground. He had put on a superb navy blue suit—coat, trousers, waistcoat—golden tie made of Banaras silk with a diamond-set tie-pin—soft patent leather shoes on his feet with a fawn-coloured spat—a high-quality felt hat on his head—as it was hot, he held lime-coloured kid gloves in his left hand and he had a leather portfolio bag in his right hand.

I guessed, as his coat did not have eighteen pockets, he had stuffed his portfolio bag with chocolates and toffees.

Soon after sunset, it started to turn purple all over, mixing the red of the sun and the azure of the sky. Its glow painted the blue waters of the Red Sea with mauve tinges. A cool soothing breeze was blowing from the Mediterranean, hundreds of miles away. The breeze was creating gentle waves in this end of the Red Sea and our launch was rocking its way through those waves. Its colour was white but it turned violet amid the palette of red, blue and purple.

The steamer was like a white-tailed swan. When swans swim, they create little white twirls; the launch's propeller was also creating many such frothy little whirlpools behind it. The propellers of big ships create such scary vicious vortices. But the small eddies of these small launches have a gentle attraction. One can stare at them for hours.

The sun set behind the Egyptian desert. Sunsets on the Padma or in the sea have their distinctiveness. Likewise, sunset in the desert too has its own charm. Bouncing on the golden sands, the sunrays invade the sky and throw a plethora of colours every minute. Even before one can comprehend the colour by comparing it to the colour of a known object, it takes on another hue. Why me? Even seasoned artists stop looking at their palette after seeing such fluctuations.

There was a British army base in Suez Port. As described by Rabi Thakur, 'The women of the Sahibs were taking their baths.' Some were riding around in small boats. The boats were of modern design, made of canvas. The structure and skeletons of the boats were built with wood and then covered with canvas. Such boats were collapsible and portable; meaning after a boat ride, the structure and the canvas cover could be taken apart, folded, put inside a bag and taken home. It would weigh less than ten kilos. But the boats were small—two people could sit inside facing each other with difficulty. They kept knick-knacks in the little empty space in the middle. I saw a pair of connoisseurs had put a small portable record player there and it was playing 'The Blue Danube'.

Such is the nature of man. Or should I call it his whims? He refuses to stay where he lives. If the pair that was playing 'The Blue Danube', was transported to the

Danube, they would start singing, 'My heart is in the Highlands; my heart is not here.'

If they were taken to the Scottish Highlands, they would sing, 'In Rosengarten von Sanssouci' meaning 'The rose garden of Sanssouci'—Sanssouci was in Potsdam close to Berlin. When taken to Germany, they would croon Indian songs. A famous poet from Germany had sung:

> On the banks of the Ganges—
> Fragrance in the air—
> The world is filled with light—
> Men and women of beauty rest
> Beneath the boughs of old trees
> All is peace and calm.

And still unsatisfied with that, they would serenade about a dreamland, a land no one had ever seen; ordinary people like us would have never come across that land; only poets could try to bring that land to earth:

> Where is the home of happiness?
> In my dreams I see it linger—
> The sun rises, the night clears—
> Like foam the dreams disappear.

I love to stay where I live. Unless it is absolutely needed, I never agree to leave my village. I have an antipathy towards travels and to visiting places. Hence I dance in joy with my hands in the air when Rabi Thakur sang in praise of our own land:

You tell me, heaven's good,
    Colours light
    The day
In Parul Danga,
        The flowers,
    With all their joy play.
Let it be great there—
    Who's taking it away?
With you, Kaki,
        Is where
    I want to stay.
That granary
          The bullock cart,
With a broken wheel rests
The branches of Gaab trees
        Flame the skies
           In red.
    Your stories, your lap
The evenings are passed.
    The owl hoots
    From Chalta trees,
As the night falls fast.
    I'll trick myself
    Out of that journey
        To heaven.
    By your side,
        My Kaki,
Is where I'll remain.

What the boy was saying, clutching his aunt, rhymed with my inner self; my body and soul felt close to it too. After travelling many countries, I had written a similar poem. As editors had declined to publish it, how could I dump it on to you now?

My senses returned with a bump. The launch had docked on the pier. But why this collision? In our Goalondo and Chandpur, ships do not dock with such jolts!

Again!

> 'On that night of the full moon
> Mind wants to make its way home.'

13

Suez Port was not to be ignored. It had military and strategic importance; hence the English had to keep part of their naval forces here. The white men, who were busy boating on the canal, looked after the base. A nice little colony had been built for them.

But it was nothing—no comparison at all to the pomp of the old days. Before the sea route around the Cape of Good Hope was discovered, or even after that, most of the goods exported from India, Burma, Java and China came on the sea and landed at Suez Port; one must not forget that in those days, the Orient exported more. The Phoenicians, and later the Greeks, then the Romans and finally the Arabs, started their journeys to India. They dumped the imported goods at Suez. They were then taken to Cairo on boats that plied on a canal. Finally, they were transported to Alexandria, Iskandria in Arabic, on the Nile river. From there they reached the whole of Europe via Venice.

A large number of Indian seamen, sailors and traders

and exporter-importers were Indians. When Vasco da Gama found the alternate route to come to India skirting around Africa, the entire business of the Orient was in the hands of the Indians and Egyptians of the Suez area.

On the one side there were the Indians and the Egyptians, on the other side the Portuguese of Vasco da Gama's descendants.

One should not refer to race hence I would like to insinuate a few things obliquely. These Portuguese goons were romping about in Goa those days; it was nothing new for them. It was in their nature. Once they were the pirates of the sea and now they are the thugs on land. This can be proved if we were to find the root of the word *bombeytay*. The word *bombeytay*, meaning pirates, did not appear from the brains of the imaginative Bengalis. *Bombeytay* originated from the Portuguese word *bombardeiro* meaning people who bombed indiscriminately without any warning. You could say that some people in Kolkata had also resorted to bombing, but their number was so small and they were so despicable that nobody had tagged the term *bombeytay* to everyone in Kolkata. But the whole of Portugal was involved in such activities and hence they became known as *bombeytay*.

Their second name in Bengali was *harmad*. That too has come from the Portuguese word 'armada'. The famous lexicographer, Gyanendra Mohan Das, has explained the origin of the word in his well-known dictionary in this way: 'The people of the Sundarbans area in the province of Bengal had to leave the region facing barbaric attacks by the Portuguese pirates. Our own poet Mukundaram had mentioned in his ballads of Chandi:

> 'White men's land wasn't near
> Nights go by in *harmads*' fear.'

Meaning the people of south Bengal in those days could not sleep at peace in fear of these *harmad*—armadas and '*bombeytay*'—*bombardeiros*.

Maybe it is now redundant, yet one could ask why did the Bengalis flee?

My reply would be, groups of marauders could land at a port or on the shore to plunder at will. It would be a difficult job if—

There was the big if—

'If' the ruler of the land deployed his navy to save his coastline. The way the kings put in place their police force to stop crime in the centres of habitation, they needed to deploy the navy to save the coastal people.

But alas, Humayun, Akbar and other Mughal rulers were then ruling Bengal. The Mughals came from the deserts of Central Asia. They had every knowledge of the theories of the use of four forces on land—infantry, cavalry, mounted elephants and camel regiments—but they were oblivious to the importance of the navy. Many desperate petitions went to them from Bengal, Orissa and Gujarat.

'Sires, please raise a naval force, or else we will lose our property, lives and honour.'

Every word of the petition was used literally. Losing 'property' meant the raids of Portuguese *bombeytay* led to destruction of the sea trade and the business of exports and imports. Losing 'lives' meant marauding and indiscriminate killings led to the closure of ports. And 'honour'? They captured the young boys and girls to sell them as slaves in the markets of Portugal.

But who was to pay them any heed? The Mughal emperors were looking to the west—towards the Khyber Pass. They came using that route, and before them the Sakas, the Huns, the Scythians, the Aryans. So they prepared the four land forces to defend the land from future invaders. To hell with the navy. India was never defeated and conquered from the sea. So why worry and spend money unnecessarily?

What was the outcome? The British trounced the Portuguese and came by the sea route to overturn the Mughals to establish their empire.

But that happened much later. We were discussing the fights that the coastal people had put up against the Portuguese. These people did not get any support from the Mughals. On the contrary, the Mughals picked fights with them.

The king of Gujarat, Bahadur Shah, was then fighting against the Portuguese. The reason being, the entire trade to Europe from north India passed through the ports of Gujarat—Surat, Broach (Vhrigu) and Khambat (Cambay). Badshah Bahadur Shah's two enemies of the time were the Portuguese in the sea and the Rajputs on land. To defeat the Rajputs first, he arranged an armistice with the Portuguese. Then he turned towards Rajputana.

The ruler of Delhi was Emperor Humayun. You must have read in history books that one Rajput woman sent a *rakhi** to Shahenshah-—the ruler of the world—Humayun. To honour the *rakhi*, Humayun moved his forces towards Rajputana. He had failed to grasp that he would not be able to tackle the Portuguese if Bahadur Shah was defeated.

Humayun was late in reaching Rajpautana. Bahadur Shah had by then conquered the land. The women of Rajpuana had committed *jauhar*†—committed suicide by jumping into burning pyres. Humayun attacked Bahadur Shah. Bahadur fled to encamp in Champani Fort. History books tell you how Humayun took over the fort. Meanwhile Bahadur was on his way to his capital, Ahmedabad. He fled towards Sourashtra, or Kathiawar, when Humayun gave him a chase. By then the Portuguese had already built bases on some of the coastal areas.

---

* Hindu ritual during the monsoon season when the sister ties an amulet on the wrist of the brother wishing him protection from harm. In turn, the brother vows to protect the sister.

† Ancient Rajput custom to save the honour of women from invaders.

Humayun suddenly received the news that the governor of Bihar, Sher Shah, was proceeding towards Delhi in a bid to capture his realm. Instantly, he turned towards Delhi. After being defeated by Sher Shah, he had to flee to take shelter in Kabul. Sher Shah remained busy trying to establish his reign in north India. So he had no time to attack Bahadur Shah. After gaining some breathing space, Bahadur said, 'Let me now tackle the Portuguese.' The Portuguese by then understood that Bahadur did not have a second front to fight any longer. So they started their old trickery. They invited Bahadur on their ship to discuss a whole gamut of agenda from the armistice to trade and business rules.

Many historians did a lot of research on why Bahadur went on board alone like a fool. No point discussing it now.

For whatever reason, the fact was, Bahadur understood that he had walked into a trap. The aim of the Portuguese was to kill him and not discuss business. He immediately jumped into the water in an attempt to swim to the shore. Following him, a couple of dozen Portuguese also jumped in the water with their oars. They smashed the skull of Gujarat's Shahenshah Bahadur Shah. With that ended India's fights against the Portuguese.

***

But why was I looking back at my country and talking about history while entering Suez Port?

It was because Bahadur had invited the king of Suez to come with his navy to join him in the sea battles against the Portuguese. I had mentioned earlier that the king of Suez knew how damaging the raids of the Portuguese pirates were for their sea trade. Not only Bahadur, but also his forefathers had invited the people of Suez repeatedly. Combining forces, they had taught the Portuguese a few good lessons too.

They had brought big cannons with them but never took them back. The Badshah of Gujarat had asked them, 'Why are you leaving them behind?' Then they had said, 'Who can tell when these Portuguese rascals will attack again? What's the point of bringing the guns again?'

Ten years after this incident, Akbar won over Gujarat. Even after seeing the cannons and knowing the history of the area, he never understood the importance of sea battles and the naval forces. Hence the Portuguese won. The English won after removing them. Gradually, after taking over Madras and Kolkata, they captured the whole of India.

***

After entering Suez Port, I remembered what a fight the people of Suez, along with us, had once put up against the Portuguese.

14

I came back to my senses. There was some commotion. We, meaning Abul Asfia's team, had been stopped by the authorities in the area. A pass was needed after landing at a port. What was the matter? Where were our health certificates? What bother! We had walked down from the motor launch all right; we were not brought down on a stretcher or on a deathbed, so what was the reason for doubting the state of our health? 'Tut, tut!' The authorities were asking for the whereabouts of the certificate that would prove that we were not carrying germs of pox, plague, cholera, tsetse fever (what was that, sir?) spotted fever (more trouble, fever with patterns?) etcetera. What was the guarantee that we would not spread those diseases in their beloved country?

Percy said, after hearing this, 'Sirs, if we were suffering from such deadly diseases, then what are we doing here without being nursed by our parents and the last sermon of the priest?'

My protégé Pratul Sen was saying, 'Why would we indulge in such treacherous acts against Egypt?'

His wife Roma was saying, 'The pyramid is your

proudest monument; like we have our Taj Mahal. Don't you think that by not allowing us in, you're depriving us of judging for ourselves which is better?'

I whispered in Roma's ears, 'So how did those people with Cook Company pass without any hitch?'

Roma said, 'Keep your mouth shut. Did you not see that they'd shown some yellow papers to them? We too have them, but in the ship.'

Oh! I remembered that while taking my passport I had to get all the inoculations and vaccinations and got a yellow-coloured certificate. So we were in such trouble because we were not carrying it with us now.

But it was not our headache. When Abul Asfia was our leader, he should have been aware that it was absolutely necessary for us to bring those faded yellow papers. One who had not common sense—

My chain of thought was disrupted. Paul was pulling me by my hand and whispering, 'Let's go back to the ship.'

But where was Abul Asfia?

We saw that he was having a smoke without any sense of worry and distributing chocolate and toffees to the people around him. A baby in his lap! God knows whose baby it was.

The man certainly was off his rocker. The advice of the good books was to desert the company of mad men.

Holding Paul's hand, I left the port office to reach the seaside. We saw that our ship, after blasting its horn, had vanished!

15

I had travelled the world. I never got flustered easily by minor mishaps. A train had left with my suitcase-trunk-holdall while I was having tea at the refreshment room. I had been penniless after losing my wallet in a foreign land. Two gangs of youths fought with knives at a restaurant in Italy while I, as an innocent harmless Bengali, was trying to save my soul by becoming a fly on the wall. All this had happened in my life a number of times, but this disaster at Port Suez because of Abul Asfia was beyond parallel.

Our ship had set off on its own course and we were stranded here because we did not have our health certificates. We now would have to stay at a hotel here and plead with every passing ship, begging for a place. Possibly we would not be allowed in. Without the health certificate they would not permit boarding the ship. It was not a 'crocodile in water and tiger on land' situation but it was more like a 'snake in water and snake on land'.

When the Japanese bombed us, I had heard this rustic song:

Do Re Me Fa So La Ti
Bombs are dropped by the Japanese
They are filled with big black snakes
'Oh my God'. Brits all quake!

Like that I felt that the Japs had dropped the snakes in the form of the health certificates both on land and in the water.

For how long would the hotel here allow us to stay? The hotel owner would surely guess the condition of our wallets and would shoo us away. Where would we go then? What would we be eating? We would be reduced to a bunch of beggars seeking alms from the rich and the poor of Port Suez. Did anyone readily open his wallet hearing someone saying, 'Please sir, I've lost all my money. If you let me have some money, I'll be able to reach home.'

Ya Allah, where did you bring us? It was like banishment to an island in the middle of the ocean.

When one can do nothing by wracking the brain, one normally tries to seek help from others. With Paul and Percy behind me, I went back to Abul Asfia.

At that point, we saw, he was asking the port officer where one could get the health certificate.

It was like the gibberish of an insane person. One could only get health certificates in one's own country; how could one get them in a foreign place?

So we could not believe our own ears when the officer replied, 'Why, in that office next door.'

Then what was the need for this tug-of-war with us? Even before we heard his answer fully, we ran to the office for our lives, as if the Japanese snakes on land and the water had started chasing us.

The door of the office was open. We saw a big-bodied man sleeping with his feet up on the table after somehow squeezing himself in a rather small chair. We surely would have heard his snoring if we were not making such a ruckus. After hearing the cacophonous music of 'our health certificates', 'our health certificates', 'please', 'please', he jumped up from his chair.

Ninety-nine per cent of passengers disembark at the port armed with their health certificates, so he spent ninety-nine per cent of his work hours in a half-dozing-half-awake state. It took him a bit of time to understand the meaning of our pitiful wailing.

We did not understand his language and he did not ours. Despite that gap, he could communicate the most devastating news that the doctor, who could check us and give us the certificates, had gone for the day.

The translation of the seven languages in which we cried would sound something like this:

'Good grief.'
'Mon Dieu, Mon Dieu.'
'Herr Gott, Herr Gott.'
'Ya Allah, Ye Khuda.'
I do not remember who else said what.

But by the mercy of God, by the unending blessings of Khuda, can anyone harm you if He wanted you alive. Thank Thee. Thank Thee. We heard the officer was saying, 'Since you people are moving about heartily and effortlessly, you will surely be healthy. I'm the one who issues the certificates. Here are the forms. Fill them up.' After saying this, he distributed a bunch of shabby brown papers among us. But they seemed so beautiful to us! It was like the school progress report and we had come first in each subject.

The way vultures start feasting on a carcass, we jumped on the forms likewise. Wrong! Linguists have cautioned against using metaphors of this horrid kind. So let me rephrase it this way, the way a mother would grab the proclamation if she was awarded the power to pardon her son who was facing execution by hanging.

In excitement and exhilaration, our brains were all jumbled. The question on the form was, 'year of birth,' and I could not remember, was it 1804 or 1704? 'Port of boarding?' Forgot it completely, was it Hong Kong or Tibet? Question, 'Destination.' What trouble, I nearly plucked the few dozen hairs left on my head but could not remember where—the planet Saturn or the star Polaris?

But we need not have worried about what we wrote on the forms. We later learned that our good-souled officer could not read a word of English.

He quickly stamped our forms with violet-coloured ink

and handed us ten certificates. Tucking them in our coat pockets like the roses of Basra, we came out in the open air. If we wished, we could now go to Cape Comorin or nowhere if we wanted it that way.

Paul said, 'Sir, I don't remember what I've written.'

I told him, 'Don't worry, brother, me neither.'

The French woman said smilingly, 'Monsieur Paul, if they had asked if I were a human or a goat, I would have first bleated for a bit and then uttered something in French to see which sounded better. Only then would I have identified myself as a human or a goat.'

After thinking for a bit, she said, 'Possibility is that it would have been a goat.'

I was hurt deeply. It was total disregard to one's own self. I said, 'Mademoiselle, I wouldn't mind if you wrote koel. Considering the sweetness of your voice—'

'Okay, okay, that's enough. Thank you!'

By that time, we had reached the railway station. We saw from a distance that the train was waiting at the platform. We increased our pace. But just as we reached the gate, the train left the station, taunting us by saying 'ta ta'.

And one man—familiar-faced—bade farewell to us by waving his hand repeatedly. Then to pretend that he was sad, he gestured to dry up the false tears in his eyes with the back of his palm.

What was the meaning of this joke?

We heard that it was the last train for Cairo that evening. If we were to catch the train the following morning, then forget seeing the city, we would not even have the time to catch the train to Port Said and would thus surely miss our ship.

After hearing this disastrous news, I collapsed on the ground with my hand on my forehead.

Why would God play with the fate of men? If we were to get stuck at Suez Port, if we were to miss the ship, it would have been all right to remain there before getting the health certificates. Why did we have to be mocked after crossing that hurdle?

I had heard of a jailer who had once left the cell door of a condemned prisoner open, leaving the way for him to flee. The prisoner thought that the jailer had forgotten to lock the door by mistake. After tiptoeing and hiding himself and evading the guards, when he stepped outside the prison to breathe fresh air, the jailer, accompanied by two guards, grabbed him. After giving him a kiss on his cheeks, the jailer said to the prisoner, 'Brother, the world is full of so much misery. You'll be relieved of it all tomorrow morning. So my friend, why were you trying to seek this false freedom tonight like a fool?'

The following morning he was hanged.

I thought, it was more severe, more harsh and way more cruel to get caught by the jailer than to get hanged.

Death is not such a harsh and severe experience.

Physicians too say that men may suffer while they are sick but they do not feel any pain at the moment of their death.

Hence Gurudev had said:

> 'Why in doubt to cross the line on your own
> Glory, glory to the unknown!'

Like this, another great man, hanged for plotting against the barbaric acts of Hitler, had written sitting in the prison,

> 'You take us through the doors of death, gently holding our hands.
> —We are moving as if in a dream—
> And suddenly we find, we are free!'

This book is for young people. They might ask why am I talking about death? I feel that one should. People may think that young people are not intelligent but I hold different opinions.

My youngest brother died at the age of two. I was thirteen then. He was a beautiful boy; he loved to sit on my lap. At that age of two, he used to sit clutching on to the bicycle's handlebar while I wheeled him round in the front yard of the house. He used to burst into laughter. Our mother looked at us with a happy face and said occasionally, 'Enough, now you take him down.'

One day he departed.

I was deeply pained.

Nobody explained to me what death was. My pain would have lessened had someone explained it to me.

Elders think that young people have fewer feelings of pain. They are wrong.

Have you people, who are reading this book, not lost a brother or a sister? One who has, will understand it.

Our poet of poets had no younger siblings. Hence I was always surprised that he could write this:

> 'Kaka says, when it's time,
> Everybody has to go
> > To Heaven's door.
> Tell me dear Kaki
> > Is that all true?
> Kaki says, before it's time,
> > Your eyelids droop,
> > The bells chime,
> By the door
> > At that time
> > The boatman comes.
> Baba left, like this
> > At dawn
> > When I was still in bed.
> Makhan left
> > Like that
> > > Late at night.'

The uncle really understood the pain of the young child.

But I have drifted from the main plot now. Let me say one more thing before coming back to the story. My faith in God is unshakable. Hence I know that when I shall cross the main gate of this world into the other, I shall see my father, grandfather, his father and other forefathers are coming forward with happy faces to receive me among them. And I know, I know it for certain, that Ma will be standing there with my brother in her lap ahead of everyone. It is even more strange when I see through the windows of my mind that this baby brother once tottered forward to receive Ma to take her to her dear ones. He had gone to that world much before her.

After I reach the other world, God will ask me, 'What do you want?' I'll instantly say 'A bicycle.' Soon after I get it, I shall put my baby brother on the cycle and wheel him round on the lawns of Heaven. He will burst into laughter. Ma will see, but will never say, 'Enough, now you take him down.'

***

The train had left. So what? There was no need to feel flustered.

We saw that Abul Asfia had vanished.

Did the man leave us behind in the middle of the sea and these unending deserts?

Coming out of the station to look for him, we saw that he was having a hearty tête-à-tête with the driver of a rickety car. We guessed that he was trying to reach Cairo by cab.

But the cab driver had, by then, understood our

doubled-edged situation. Seeing an opportunity, he asked for a fare with which he could buy a new car.

Abul Asfia narrated many stories of religion to him; he praised the Indo-Egyptian friendship to the hilt; he told him that he was a Muslim and so was the cabbie and finally he swore on the mores of the truth; but the cabbie, despite being a Muslim, proved to be a true villain. Without a battle, he was refusing to move even an inch.

There was no sign of anger on Abul Asfia's face. With a Zen-like face he proceeded to the Health Office. I started following him.

The bulky gentleman who had rescued us from our initial trouble by giving us the health certificates, was back to his nap by then. Abul Asfia and I had to put in a lot of effort to wake him up.

The gist of what Abul Asfia told him was something like this: he was not afraid of robbers; he knew how to pull his gun if the robber showed his; but he did not have weapons to fight such robbery without any guns; he could surely find a way but we would be obliged and he would be blessed by God if he came to our assistance.

The office said, 'Let's go.'

After talking to the cabbies, he settled the fare. We calculated that it was equal to the first-class train fare to Cairo. We were happy. We would reach Cairo and then we would be able to catch our ship from Port Said. There was no more worry.

We filled into two taxis like sardines in a tin.

Before getting into the taxi, I thanked him by saying, 'You did so much for us. You are indeed a very kind person.'

I was gobsmacked hearing his reply in broken English. He said that there was not an iota of kindness in him. He did not extend any helping hand to us. If a bunch of beggars like us got stranded in Suez Port then we would become their headache. So he was relieved to get rid of us, etc.

I was about to take my seat in the taxi, when suddenly it dawned on me—I remembered an incident.

The repository of all Tagore's songs was Dinendranath, the grandson of his elder brother. My artist friend Binodbihari had once borrowed his binoculars. Binod unfortunately had bad eyesight. After a few days when he went to return it, Dinendranath asked, 'How did you see through it?'

'Fabulous.' Binod had never seen anything so clearly.

'Then you keep it. People really annoy me by asking for it all the time. Someone asks for it one day, another the following and a third person the day after that. I can't manage. It's best if it stays with you.'

Binod tried several times but could never return the binoculars.

This is the way of truly generous people to help others. They show that they never extended a helping hand. They pretend that they have done so for their own sake, very selfishly.

I understood that the officer belonged to the same species as Dinendranath. I used the term 'species' deliberately. My belief is that all kind souls—be they Brahmin or Chandal, Hindu or Muslim, African or Nordic—are of a single species.

By then we had entered the desert by leaving the port behind. Looking back, I saw the city lights dwindling away the way old memories fade with age.

16

Moonlight on the desert. It was a sublime sight. It was not possible to have such a sight in the green surroundings in Bengal. If ever you had to venture onto the sandbars in the middle of the Padma during the full moon—Rabindranath often used to do this and his '*Nisheethe*' or 'At Night' story had been written with that backdrop—you would get some taste of it.

The whole experience is spooky. Your eye is moving up to the horizon but then is suddenly obstructed by the mesh of a faded screen. It appears as though you can see it but actually not quite. It looks familiar but not quite. In the desert, white moonlight was oozing all around; it felt that one could read the newspaper in that illumination but could not differentiate between black and red. On a cloudy day, such differences were far more visible.

Hence:

> As if a bird, as if a cloud or a young tree
> But none is there when I try to see.
> Are these castles or tree roots
> Or is it a sky, full of my illusions?

At times there were two green blobs of light blinking two feet above the car's height. What were they? Were they eyes of ghouls? I had heard that eyes of ghosts were green. No. When they came close, we saw that it was a caravan of camels—in the local language it was called *kafila* (the poet Kazi Nazrul Islam has used that word in his writing). The headlight of the car fell on the camels' eyes, turning them into green blobs. I am used to seeing the illuminated eyes of cattle in our land but the eyes of the camels were at least two feet higher than the car, which is why I was spooked.

And why would I not be? We were passing though the desert roads at night, yes, repeating it again—at night—where there was not a single soul. I had read so many stories—true or false—about the deserts since my childhood. The Bedouin died there in thirst; to save his life he cut the throat of his camel that he loved more than his own son and quenched his thirst by drinking the water stored inside its throat; turning mad in the heat, he would take all his clothes off and looking at the sun, he sang in a hoarse broken voice,

> What can you do to me—who are you?
> You (swear words)—who are you?
> And even more ugly poems without any rhythm.

What if the car broke down? What if no cars came this way till the following evening? I had seen clearly that the car did not load twenty-five gallons of water before setting off. What would happen then?

But by God's grace, I saw that Paul and Percy were made of different mettle. Overshadowing the wheezing, whistling, whimpering, wailing noise of the rickety car, they were bellowing even louder. How happy they were!

Paul: 'See everything in great detail. We need to write to Mother properly.'

Percy: 'You are right for the first time. Let's make sure we leave out nothing. Blimey, we're driving through the desert. When we boarded the ship, did we ever think that we would get the chance to travel through the desert?'

Paul: 'Right-o. Just think how surprised Father and Mother will be? But what if they scold us? What if they ask why we had to go on this adventure leaving the ship? Then what?'

Percy: 'This is the trouble with you. Always anxious and doubtful. Won't we be able to find a suitable answer then? Sir is sitting here. Ask him and see what he says.'

I said, 'It can be dealt with if they at all find you at fault. Why you are you missing the opportunity of seeing what is around us now by discussing that eventuality? Especially when we can't undo anything about what we've already done even if it was wrong.'

Percy quipped, 'And what's the point of going back? Our ship has left a long time ago.'

The boy was clever; he had ready wit.

In the desert, days were terribly hot; likewise the nights were equally cold. Scientists gave some well-researched explanation of this phenomenon; I couldn't say, without any experiment, how acceptable the theory was. Right now I could only say, in the unbearable heat on the ship, our flesh and bones had dried up like pickles. Here, after getting the magical touch of the cold air, they flourished like jasmine flowers.

I had had a similar experience more than once. After passing through 120 to 122 degrees in Peshawar and Jalalabad, my body and mind had been soothed when I reached the 60 degrees in Khak-e-Jabbar. I had described that in another book. Which one? No, not saying it. People will say I am inserting a free advertisement for my book here.

I did not know for how long I had slept. I saw rows of lights ahead when I was woken up by the sudden jerking of the car. We had reached Cairo. Everyone in the cab was sleeping. I thought possibly the driver was too. The car was moving on its own towards its garage like a horse without a rider finds his stable.

I woke up Percy with a nudge and said, 'So my brother, didn't you say that you had to see everything on the way in the desert and make notes in the notebook of your mind?' I pretended as if I had stayed awake.

Percy was equally indomitable. He instantly yanked Paul's ear and repeated what I told him. What could poor

Paul do? He gently woke up Mademoiselle Chenier and said to her, 'We have reached Cairo.'

In Bengal there is a saying, 'The man of the house slapped his wife, the wife struck the maid with a stick, the maid kicked the cat and the cat scratched the sack of salt.'

This was the law of the world.

But the adage here was not followed entirely. Paul woke up the French lady gently.

Mademoiselle took out the powder puff from her handbag and asked in French—my suspicion is French women can apply lipstick even in their sleep—'Where have we reached, monsieur?'

'Le Caire.'

Paul knew French rather well. He asked me, '"Le Caire" is "The Cairo". Also Le denotes the masculine gender. How can one assign gender identity to a city?'

I replied, 'I don't have much knowledge. But I know that the French are not the only culprits in this regard. In our language, we refer to the Brahmaputra river as male and the Ganges as a female. I don't know why we say it like that.'

Percy added, 'And why do we, the English, call a ship "she"?'

I said, 'For the time being let's hand this debate over to Oxford. You're going there to study anyway. Right now, enjoy the beauty of Cairo by night.'

True, such beautiful sights were not encountered daily.

When we approached Kolkata from Chandannagar, we normally would not grasp the grandeur of Kolkata because of thick built-up areas in between and its brightly lit lights. But here we saw all those city lights all of a sudden after crossing the desert, giving a mirage-like impression.

Atop a six-storeyed building—but the building was not visible—I saw the neon-lit needle, in red light, of a sewing machine was going up and down rapidly and its wheel in green light was circling non-stop. The name of an English company was written at the bottom. I thought, alas! Had the name of the machine been 'Usha'. That day will come when our Indian...but let it be.

So many such neon advertisements. Kolkata's neighbourhoods sleep at eleven. The eyes of Cairo were open even now—we could see lights inside the windows. And less we talk about the streets, the better it would be. So many restaurants, so many cafés, so many shops in this suburb were open; they were filled with customers. The way we have our tea stalls, Egyptians similarly have their cafés. I sometimes think if coffee shops can be called café, then why can we not call our tea stalls cha-fe? 'Okay brother, let's go to cha-fe for a cup of cha?'

I will repeat again, it was eleven. I had seen many cities that stayed up late but I never saw a night owl like Cairo.

The aroma of the cuisines of Cairo was hanging over the streets. Even a whiff would tempt you to make a stop and taste some of it. But the restaurants were as dirty as our eateries. But did that matter? Someone had said, 'Dirty restaurants serve the best food. Doesn't the black cow produce white milk?'

I had no objection to eat here. But what about these sahibs and memsahibs? They would possibly utter 'Mon Dieu,' 'Herr Gott' and many such things.

Suddenly both cars stopped. We started having cramps after sitting in one position for such a long time. All of us got off. Everyone had the same intention—to stretch a little, to take a few steps, to extend the hands.

At that moment, Abul Asfia, standing amidst us with his head tilted behind a little and spreading both his hands in front, started giving a politician-like lecture, like the ones we heard at Shraddhananda Park, in his broken French,

'Madam, mademoiselle et monsieur...

'We all are thirsty and hungry by now. After entering the city, the first thing we'll do is eat and drink in some good or average restaurant. But the question is, what can they offer? The same as we get on the ship. The same bland soup, blander stew and blandest pudding. Meaning, be it Anglo-Indian or Anglo-Egyptian, the same food devoid of any taste.

'On the contrary, if we are to eat the most authentic, unadulterated Egyptian food, well cooked in Egyptian recipes, won't we have a new experience?'

Even before we said anything, he folded his arms and said while scratching his right neck with his left hand,

'But of course, these restaurants look dirty. The tables and chairs are not clean; but madam, mademoiselle et monsieur, we're not going to eat the chairs and tables. We'll eat their food. As the ship's meals couldn't kill us, what can this food do? You give your verdict.'

Before anyone said anything, Percy cried out, 'Of course, of course, we'll eat here. When we're breathing Egyptian air, then why can't we eat Egyptian food and drink Egyptian drinks?'

Mademoiselle Chenier said, 'People who don't want to, may not eat here. I'm going in.'

I realized how free France was. Freedom was ingrained in the marrows of the French people.

Chenier was the most delicate among us. She did not like the food on the ship; hence she survived by eating only toast, milk, coffee and boiled eggs.

In my belief, all us did not enter the eatery post-haste because Mademoiselle Chenier showed us the way, but we were equally ready to taste Egyptian delicacies. The main reason was of course, everyone was terribly hungry. No one knew when we would reach a restaurant of pedigree and neither did we know how much time it would take. Instead, the food full of aroma was lot better. One should be happy with whatever one has in hand.

Rabindranath said,

> Why flout the love nearby
> In search of fantasy?

The Iranian poet Omar Khayyam too had uttered,

> Oh, take the cash, and let the credit go.
> Nor heed the rumble of a distant drum!

***

The waiters of the restaurants raced up to welcome (*Istikbal*) us. The 'boys' grinned, showing all their thirty-two teeth. Quickly they pulled and joined up three small tables and arranged chairs around them for us to sit; the chef, with the towel on his shoulder, came running from the kitchen and started to bow before us repeatedly. Taking my seat, I realized that it was the same iron chair of our cafés in Shyambazar—they sting both in summer and in winter.

By then, I was immersing myself in the surroundings. Meaning, I was appreciating the perfect teeth of the 'boys'. From where did they get such milk-white teeth? In front of the teeth, how did they manage to have such pink lips? And a soft dark shade had spread all over their bodies. It was not our dusky colour, it was more of a bronze tinge. How smooth, how beautiful!

But the best sight was the belly of the chef. Oh! What size, what breadth, how imposing!

I guessed from seeing it that we had entered the right restaurant.

Meanwhile Abul Asfia and Mademoiselle Chenier had vanished inside the kitchen with the chef to take a look and choose the food. And a quartet of young boys surrounded us shouting, 'Booth bolish, booth bolish.'

It did not take long for me to decipher the meaning because they were carrying small boxes and two pairs of brushes with them. Going through the theories of phonetics my mind understood, as there was no pronunciation of T in the Arabic language, 'boot' had become 'booth'; similarly there was no letter in Arabic for P; so 'polish' had become 'bolish'. So 'booth bolish' meant 'boot polish'. This was the reason the Arabs called Pundit Nehru as Bundith Nehru. Lucky they could not pronounce T, or else Nehru would have become a 'Bandit'. In the Arabic of Aden region, there was no letter for 'G' and hence people there called 'Gandhi' as 'Jandi'. But no harm there—he had given up his life (*jaan di*) to uphold truth.

Bengalis spend hours in front of the mirror to style their hair. The Englishman repeatedly makes sure that his tie is in the middle of his neck. The Sikhs take an hour to tie their turbans. The Kabulis always get the cobbler to put a few nails on the sole of their shoes. Similarly, I saw that the residents of Cairo were intoxicated by 'booth bolish'. Or else why would dozens of 'booth bolish' boys raid restaurants in the middle of the night?

But true, they knew how to polish shoes. They removed the old polish with spirit, washed all dirt with soap and water, applied cream, put in a fresh touch of polish, and then shined the shoes first with canvas cloth and finally with silk. The shoes were so shiny that one could easily see one's face on it. They did not use the brush at all, apparently it damaged the leather.

What surprised me most was that at the end, using a piece of cloth, they took the sheen off the super-shiny shoes—but only a little. Why? After putting in so much work to shine the shoe, why did they have to take the gloss off?

I remembered a story.

An Englishman ordered a birthday cake at a bakery. The baker was supposed to put the initials of his name, P.B.W., on the cake in golden and blue. While taking delivery, the man told the baker, 'The cake looks beautiful but the writing on top is in straight letters. I want them to be in italics with a floral design.'

The baker wanted to appease his customer. He said, 'I'll change it just now. It's a birthday after all.'

With a lot of labour, he first scraped the top of the cake. Then he sweated to put the initials in italics and covered the cake with a floral decoration around it.

The man was happy. He said, 'It is perfect.'

The baker asked, 'Shall I pack it or send it to any special address?'

The Englishman said with a smile, 'None of it. I'll eat it here.'

Then he cut the cake in pieces and ate it all.

The baker was stumped. What was the need to do all of it?

The same rule applied for 'booth bolish' too.

I asked the 'booth bolish' boy the meaning of taking the sheen off the shined shoes.

He was confused at first. Then he replied, 'Only the uncultured people would like to keep their shoes too shiny. The refined people have a different taste for everything.'

O-h-h-!

I remembered, Aban Tagore[*] had mentioned that when the women of the Tagore family went out in their palanquin, they used to cover their jewellery with a wrap of fine muslin. A shiny show-off was the hallmark of philistines.

---

[*] Abanindranath Tagore, nephew of Rabindranath Tagore, one of the most notable painters of Bengal in the early to mid-twentieth century. A prominent writer of children's books as well.

17

Our Bengali meals consist of five flavours of food—bitter, savoury, hot, sour sides and desserts. The English eat only sweet and savoury preparations. They cannot stomach the hot stuff, and even less the sour. And possibly never even knew that bitters could be consumed. Hence English cuisine seems bland and tasteless to us. But the English can bake good cake-pastry-pudding, something they learned from the Italians. In my opinion, our *sandesh* and *rasogolla* are such delicacies that there is no reason to go bananas over those desserts.

Egyptian cuisine is a close cousin of Indian food of the Mughlai variety. I might not be able to prove the theory but after tasting food in many countries, it is my firm belief that imitating the Taj Mahal of cooking, that the Mughals perfected after coming to India (one should not forget that they could not master it in their own land as the Indian spices were unavailable in their motherland of Turkestan), the people in Afghanistan, Iran, the Arab land, Egypt, even Spain, have been trying to build their own little Taj of cuisine. The reach of this gastronomy has spread to East Europe's Greece, Hungary, Rumania, Yugoslavia, Albania and even Italy.

I discovered all these theories many years later. At present Abul Asfia and Claudette Chenier brought back samples of various dishes on a platter. I saw there was *murg musallam, sheesh kebab* and five or six kinds of unknown items. The known ones did not really carry the aroma of Kolkata food but it mattered little. After eating Irish stew and Italian macaroni on the ship, our palates had lost all taste; so seeing these dishes made our mouths water. My heart was craving for a little boiled rice, fried bitter gourd, *sonamoog daal* or yellow lentil, fried *potol** and fish curry—why was I daydreaming? Just rice and fish curry could do, but these were not available outside Bengal. So what was the point of such mourning?

So I showed them the items from the platter I did not want.

Peeking at the next table, I saw one man was about to start eating two cucumbers on a plate. How could two cucumbers, whatever the size might be, be enough for someone's dinner? I could not solve that puzzle by wracking my brain. That too, he was sitting at a table in an eatery supplemented by sauces and chutneys. Even in a sophisticated country like England, people would bite

---
* Pointed gourd.

into an apple right after buying it off the street. They did not have to enter a restaurant to eat it with a fork and knife with sauces and chutneys. Was this country more sophisticated than England? Or were there strange laws here that forbade people to eat cucumbers on the street? Just like our nonsensical rhyme about the country of Lord Shiva:

> If you trip and come a cropper,
> you're collared by the nearest copper,
> the magistrates upon you seize,
>   and fine you twenty-one rupees.
> You also need a special lease
> till six o'clock to cough or sneeze,
> and those who sneeze without permission
> are thrashed in gentle admonition,
> and twenty-one compelling doses
> of snuff rammed up their streaming noses.[*]
> Who could tell what the food was?

At that point I saw, instead of chewing the cucumber, the man just pressed it in the middle and some pulau-like substance mixed with a few things oozed out. I was surprised to no end. I told the restaurant owner that whatever be my luck, I ought to eat those cucumbers.

Two cucumbers were served. After pressing them a

---

[*] 'Ekushe Ain' by Sukumar Ray: Translation by Sukanta Chaudhuri in *Select Nonsense of Sukumar Ray* (Oxford; 1997).

little with a fork, the pulau came out. The pulau was mixed with small pieces of meat (what we call *keema*), slices of tomato and grated country cheese. I realized that all the stuffings had been put inside the boiled cucumber and finally it was fried in ghee. The same principle as our *dolma* of fish and *potol*—the only difference was here they had stuffed the cucumber with pulau, meat, tomato and cheese. Thus this was a truly superlative creation.

And what taste! It melted the moment it touched my tongue.

I had never eaten such a five-in-one dish.

I also tasted another unique item—Egyptian broad bean seeds. You must have seen the massive kegs of oil in the Alibaba film. In two or three such kegs, they put broad bean seeds and boil them overnight. After adding olive oil and some spices, they serve them from the morning. We ate them at midnight. What taste! I can still feel it in my mouth. Our pumpkin seeds are no match for this delicacy. Even Paul and Percy agreed that the soybeans of China would be far behind, never mind surpassing it.

We heard that the king and the poor—everyone ate those beans twice a day. The restaurant owner told us that some pharoah liked it so much that he had forbidden his subjects to eat these beans! Hence the reason why people talk about the whims of the pharaohs.

I picked up its Arabic name—*fool*.

The following is an incident from the following

morning but as it is related to this item, I will narrate it here.

Dozens of nationalities like the French, the Greeks, the Italians, the English lived in Cairo. So the city was adorned with signage in languages from around the world. The following morning when we were exploring the nooks and crannies of the city, I came across a signboard that said:

Fool's Restaurant

Paul, Percy and I noticed it together. We were lost for words and finally we burst out laughing.

'A restaurant for stupid people?'

What did it really mean?

At that point I suddenly remembered the word *fool* had been used in Arabic for the broad bean dish. Not meaning stupid people. It meant this shopkeeper sold broad bean seeds. The three of us peeped inside the shop to see that all the customers had a plate of *fool* in front of them.

***

You all laughed I suppose.

So did I.

But many years later, after returning to Kolkata, I noticed a signboard on which was written:

Kopir Singara

Meaning samosa stuffed with cauliflower. Right?

But if I decided to understand the other meaning of

kopi as monkey, then the meaning would be 'samosa for monkeys'. It would mean that people who went to that shop to eat samosa were monkeys, like the way we thought only stupid people went to 'Fool's Restaurant'.

People, for generations, have created such funny advertisements knowingly or unknowingly—possibly more unknowingly. One nephew of mine collated a cache of such funny ads with pictorials. The hobby was not bad. One of them read like this:

> Aurginal Bramvan's Hotalry
> Phish—Four anna
> Mitty—Eight anna
> Vaggies—Six anna

Let that be. Now back to Cairo. After finishing dinner, we got into our cars again. I saw that Abul Asfia fed the drivers from his own pocket. After getting into the car, he said to them, 'You have no permit to drive taxis in Cairo. But we have brought you here from outside. So you can easily make some extra cash by taking us around.'

Hearing the generous proposal, they were immensely glad. But the *fool* in their tummy jumped up to their throat hearing the price that Abul Asfia suggested for driving us around.

The upshot was that Abul Asfia had by then found out the price for hiring taxis in Cairo—how much they charged per mile and he was proposing far less than that to these cabbies. He now had them under his control. When they protested vigorously, he said with a tone of feigned sympathy, 'So brothers, don't come with us if you don't want to. I can't force you to take us around. If you think you've earned enough and you don't want to make more, then I can't force you. Even Allah has said, "To be content is a virtue."'

Then, releasing a deep sigh, he said, 'So brothers, we'll book other taxis. You return to Suez. Allah be with you always, let his Prophet bless you. But brothers, we had such a pleasant time with you for the last few hours.'

Pleasant time? My foot. If he had his way, Abul Asfia would have beheaded them.

I was surprised to see the man's pretence. What acting he could produce just to save a few bob!

And how he cooed like a pigeon! On the ship, the same man had his mouth shut in a way that it felt as if his words were strictly rationed.

Finally the cabbies agreed, not at the rate suggested by Abul Asfia but for a slightly higher rate.

'Pyramids,' Abul Asfia commanded in a regal tone. By then we had entered Cairo's city centre.

Kolkata's midnight could never come close to that of Cairo. Scores of restaurants, hotels cinemas, dance halls, cabarets were open. The whole city was thriving with customers of all sorts.

And people of so many origins.

There were the most authentic black Africans. They had curly black hair like the wool of a lamb, two deep red thick lips, Nubian noses, teeth like white seashells; and the beauty of their black skin was unique. I knew that they did not moisten their bodies with oil but it seemed that oil was seeping from under their skin. Their skin was so well oiled, so polished that mosquitos or flies would slip if they tried to sit on their bodies, breaking their six legs in compound fractures; they would have to spend six months in the hospital encased in plaster.

Then you could see the Sudanese people. Everyone was six-foot tall. As they were wearing long robes, they looked even taller. Their skin was bronze-coloured. Their lips were not thick or red like that of the black Africans. But the most prominent sight was the length of their arms. Their arms stretched almost to their kneecaps.

Sri Ramachandra's arms reached his knees and his skin colour was like that of the newly formed monsoon clouds or newly grown Bermuda grass. So did that mean unless you had bronze-coloured skin you would not have long arms? Did that also mean that people with fair skins had short arms and people with darker skin types had long arms? At some point, I would have to put that question to an anthropologist.

Suddenly we saw that there was a commotion ahead of us. The place was jam-packed with people.

There were so many people on the road that our cars

had to come to a halt. Paul and Percy jumped atop the hood of the car before I could ask them not to do it. They wanted to witness what was happening in the crowd. I was past the age for such inquisitiveness. Mademoiselle Chenier was keen on getting off too; I asked her not to venture out.

Meanwhile, the police came mounted on horses and dispersed the crowd. As a result, our cars moved. Paul and Percy came down from the hood and took seats on either sides of me.

I did not have to ask them what happened. Their excitement was uncontrollable. They were talking at the same time. Finally I asked Paul to keep quiet and said to Percy, 'Percy, you tell us what happened.'

'You saw those Sudanese men; one of them was holding a white soldier by his collar with his left hand and slapping him with the other. The white man could do nothing, as the long arm of the Sudanese had kept the soldier at such a distance that his attempted blows did not reach his face. It went on like that for two-three minutes. Then the police came and took the white man away after arresting him.'

I asked, surprised, 'The Sudanese was beating him, but he wasn't arrested? How come they arrested the man who was being beaten up and not the man who was beating him?'

Paul and Percy said in unison, 'That was the funny bit, sir. In a place like Shanghai if anyone beat up a white man, he would be arrested after being thrashed properly. Nobody would even ask who the guilty party was.'

I then asked our driver to solve the riddle.

The driver said, 'Sudanese people work as guards in this country. People of Cairo have unending trust in them. I wouldn't be able to vouch that no Sudanese man had ever committed any treachery, but at least I've never heard of any such incident. They are extremely religious. They pray five times a day, fast during Ramadan, go to the Haj and take God's name by counting rosary beads. And they guard the houses where they are employed. This Sudanese man slapping the white man was the doorkeeper of a restaurant. Finishing a meal there, the white soldier tried to give the slip without paying. The owner got a punch after challenging him. So the Sudanese guard was merely doing his job. After asking around once, the police believed the Sudanese guard and arrested the white man. Everyone knows that the Sudanese men are peace-loving and quiet types; they don't get involved in fisticuffs.'

At last we understood everything. But I needed to admit that only a Sudanese could beat up an English soldier alone, without any help from anybody. I did not know if a Pathan could do that. He might, but as his arm was not as long as the Sudanese, he would surely receive a few blows in return.

It rained in Cairo only once in a while. That too, not more than an inch or two. So everyone was sitting out on the verandas or the terraces of the cafés and hotels. I learned that cinema shows too take place in the open air.

In our land of Bengal, we spend a lot time in the local tea shops chinwagging. Some people go to the same shop everyday to spend a couple of hours but the habit of spending most of the day at cafés started from the Frontier. In Kabul, you will see four friends trying to reach the *chai-khana*, negotiating snow-covered roads, to have some idle chitchat—as if this could not be done at home. If asked, they will say, 'Elders are present at home; nobody knows when they will come and scold one of us. Alternately they may even say, "Son Firoz Bakt, please go to your uncle's house (a matter of a two and half miles) to tell him that the boil on my nose is on the mend and he shouldn't worry much about it. And you see, on your way back, can you go to the laundry woman and ask her (another detour of a mile and a half) if my blue robe, etc etc. etc."

'The main reason is that women of the house, grandmother, mother or aunts refuse to supply pots of tea all day long. It's not as if they're spendthrift. If I tell my eldest aunt that my friends have come and they have expressed their desire to have the lamb roast—stuffed with minced meat pulao and chicken stuffed with big fish, the one you had cooked on the occasion of the youngest aunt's wedding, then she'll start cooking it immediately. It is of no consequence if that cost her ten or twenty rupees.

'In comparison, how much would it cost to make a few pots of tea? A quarter of a rupee or half a rupee at most? That's not the point. If you drink too many cups of tea in one go, you'll lose your appetite, you won't be able to have your meal.

'So you see, brother, the tea shop is the best option. There's no fear of getting scolded by the elders once you've taken your seat in the tea shop. You don't have to go to your uncle's house to deliver the bulletin of the boil on father's nose; here you can get barrels of tea; you can meet a few close friends; you can play chess or cards here too. So where else can we go if not here?'

It was not as if the first Kabuli gentleman I met elaborated all that but upon enquiring with many people I gathered the reasons for going to the tea shops.

I had no doubt that they were telling me the truth, and there should not be any objection for them to throng the tea shops.

But these reasons are valid in the case of Bengalis too. Our mothers and aunts do not want us to drink too many cups of tea; our fathers and uncles are equally keen on assigning some sort of work to us; why then did we not turn the tea shops into our living rooms?

I was yet to get a proper answer to this question. But at present, I noticed that the natives of Cairo were most adept at spending time at cafés until midnight or even one in the morning; the gathering at home dispersed after ten or eleven at night as the rest of the family would finish dinner and get ready to go to bed. That possibility was absent here. Saying that they were leaving many times, nobody actually left. The families became used to it too. They made some other arrangements. I heard that some cafés here opened at midnight.

The car crossed the roads quickly and so I could not see everything properly. But now a most soothing sight appeared before our eyes. The Nile!

I am a son of East Bengal. Just any river cannot impress me so easily. If the creator of the universe had not woven a tapestry with hundreds of rivers in East Bengal, how could the Bhatiyali* song come about? I often contemplated that He had painted the canvas and we created Bhatiyali, of course by borrowing the idea from Him. When we stretched the tune of a Bhatiyali song, did we not see the calm river was flowing serenely to its tune, the waters ebbing and flowing with the rhythm of the song?

It was not possible for me to carry thousands of rivers on my shoulders to the discerning people of Paris and Vienna but I could play a good record of Bhatiyali music to them.

Stupidly I did that once. And you should listen to how I had to pay for it dearly.

In Vienna, a Russian man used to stay in the room

---

* Songs of boatmen of Bengal.

next to mine. He had come there to learn continental music. Vienna was the workplace of Beethoven, Mozart—they were in the same league as Tansen, Thyagaraja, and Rabindranath and Nazrul of us Bengalis.

Vienna was situated on the banks of the Danube. Some of you might have heard the composition 'Blue Danube'.

One day the Russian commented, 'The Danube or whatever is no river at all. How can this river inspire songs that will compete with our Volga and the emotions of the songs created by its boatmen? Do you believe in God or some other creator? I don't. I can clearly see Nature. Its mellifluousness is expressed in the shape of rivers. And we beat it with the melodies of the boatmen of the Volga.'

After returning home, he played a record of the songs of boatmen of the Volga. In full appreciation I said, 'Beautiful.'

By then my Bangal* blood started heating up. Only a Bangal will know what that means. The Ghoti—meaning the people of West Bengal often make a mockery of us. I never take any offence to that. They love our Bhatiyali and we are mad about their Baul songs.

My Bangal blood was boiling and I started saying, 'There are hundreds of rivers in our land of Bengal. How many rivers are there in Russia? Volga is one of the few. That will beat all our rivers in Bengal? Let me prove it.'

---

* People of East Bengal.

Luckily I had a record of Abbasuddin's *'Rangila Naiyyer Majhi'*. Instantly I played it on the gramophone to the Russian.

He listened to it with his eyes closed. After that what he said meant, 'Fraud.'

I asked, 'What do you mean?'

He said, 'The tune is of a superior category but more striking is its originality. I admit with folded hands that I haven't heard any music like this before. But I'll also say, this is not folk music; because so many notes can't be heard in any form of folk music anywhere in the entire world. Hence I'm saying it's a fraud.'

I said, 'My son, that's the beauty of Bhatiyali songs. The way its notes go up and down, no other folk music does it.'

He refused to accept that it was folk music. His opinion was that it was hanging in the limbo in between folk and classical music and within a few years some expert would ordain it as 'high-class' music.

One day he finally accepted that it was folk music. Courtesy the BBC. While presenting folk music from around the world, the BBC played a Bhatiyali song after announcing that it was a folk song from East Bengal.

I won the battle but I started paying for it dearly. It might sound strange that the person who won, was having to pay for it. It happened and was still happening. The American and the British won the war in Germany and are still paying a lot of money there. Whatever it was, let me explain how I had to pay by winning the bet.

Since then, whenever he wanted to punish me, he played Bhatiyali on his violin.

Do you understand my condition? In a foreign land, I was already terribly homesick. To top it off, there was the most heart-rending tunes of Bhatiyali!

Like Srikantha babu of Rabindranath, I would plead with him with teary eyes to stop playing his violin.

But I will admit even now, the way that man could play Bhatiyali music on his violin, it was sublime.

I have travelled to so many countries, got love and affection from so many people unknown to me, was abused at times, saw the rise and fall of a man like Hitler. I may have forgotten profound experiences but I cannot forget such insignificant memories. It seems that they happened just a few hours before.

***

In the moonlight I saw that a medium-sized trading boat was sailing, slightly tilted with its triangular sail swollen like the belly of an overeating greedy boy. There was little breeze but like a glutton the sail had gorged all of it and swollen its belly. One feared that if the wind picked up, the sail could burst easily or, getting a push from behind, the boat would capsize after doing two vaults and disappear into the depths of the Nile.

Agriculture in this country happened with the waters of the Nile. This Nile also carries the produce to other parts of Egypt. Hence the poet of this country had sung:

I love thee oh Nile-flooded earth
Thy love is my religion, my labour.

18

Pyramid! Pyramid!! Pyramid!!!

We use three exclamation marks when we want to express utter surprise. Was the reason that there were three pyramids standing in front of us? Or was it the other way round? Our surprises were expressed three times because there were three pyramids?

So many books have been written on these pyramids all over the world that it would be equal to this one, if I attempted to list all such publications. It is because these three pyramids are the oldest standing monuments in the world. People have stood in front of them through the ages trying to guess what was inside; they tried to decipher the glyphs etched on their walls in a bid to get information about them; and as you may know, for six and a half thousand years, people had attempted to reach the treasure rooms hidden inside them. After conquering this country, the Persians, Greeks, Romans, Arabs, Turks, French, English—everyone's first endeavour was to try to loot the treasures hidden in the deepest cellar, by getting inside the structures made of thousands of tonnes of rock. But the most fascinating fact was that the person who reached the hidden room first had no intention of looting it. He had entered purely to seek historical knowledge. The masons of the pharaohs had blocked the entrance to the treasure room with a massive piece of rock and plastered it in such a way that it took people more than six thousand years to gain entry into it.

There are other pyramids inside and outside Egypt but the three pyramids of Giza that we saw are world-famous—one of the Seven Wonders of the World.

Pharoah	Period of construction	Length on ground	Height
Khufu	4700 BC	755 feet	481 feet
Khafre	4600 BC	706 feet	471 feet
Menkaure	4550 BC	346 feet	210 feet

It is impossible to gauge the height of the pyramid only by saying it is nearly five hundred feet high. It is difficult to comprehend how tall it is when one sees it up front. Instead of tapering off gradually for five hundred feet starting from a massive square base, had it stood keeping the same dimensions, the massive height would have been more apparent.

It can be grasped if we move away from it. Even travelling far from Giza and Cairo, they can be seen standing tall, above everything. And if one decides to venture into the deserts, it seems that the pyramids are visible from the other edge of the Sahara!

Only then can we know why two million three hundred thousand stones were needed to build this structure. It would be an understatement if one merely said stone, as four or five of them joined together would be as large and as heavy as a rail engine. Or, if these stones measuring six feet by three were aligned together, they would make a six-hundred-fifty-mile-long wall. Such a wall would stretch from Kolkata to Darjeeling and come back again.

Apparently it took one hundred thousand people twenty years to build the biggest of the pyramids.

Imagine the wealth and the influence of the ruler who could house and feed one hundred thousand people right next to his capital. Leave aside the questions of other expenses, the task of organizing the housing and feeding of one hundred thousand workers and sustaining it for twenty years proves the height of civilization they had attained.

And why did they build the pyramids?

Everyone knows the primary reason. The pharaohs believed that they would not pass into an eternal life if their bodies decomposed after they died or they had injuries on their bodies. Hence their dead bodies were mummified and preserved inside a strong pyramid so that nobody could get in to tamper with them. But alas, their wishes were not fulfilled. I had stated before that after trying for thousands of years, the bad guys (the looters) and the good people (the scholars) eventually entered their secret crypts. That way the wishes of some of the pharaohs came true—the scholars moved their mummies for safekeeping to some museums. The pharaohs will be waiting there for the final day of apocalypse after which they can start their eternal afterlife with a new and young body.

But what if there is another World War? If a few atom bombs fell? Then?

My belief is that as they had been saved for thousands of years from the thieves, robbers, rich people and scholars, they will surely reach the final day of the destruction. I would rather take up a position close to one of them if there is ever a possibility of an atom bomb. The mummy, like a shield, will save his body as well as mine. Even the city might be saved.

I had mentioned the second reason for building the pyramids at the beginning of the chapter.

The pharaohs wanted to proclaim the heights of civilization they had attained, the powerful kingdoms they had established, and that these would remain indestructible and unchanged like the pyramids. 'There will be no change'; 'it will remain as it is'; these were the second reasons for building pyramids. Like an immobile Colossus, in a literal sense, the pyramids keep their established empires, dynasties and religious norms intact for ages without changing them.

Hence people are fearful seeing the pyramids. They feel intimidated—as if the pharaohs are still alive. People would not have dared to go against the wishes of the person who had had the pyramids built.

The sheer poetry of the Taj Mahal will moisten the stony heart of a hardened person. The upright spine of the Qutub Minar teaches a weakling how to stand up straight. These two fine senses of aesthetics are at the heart of poetry and music. One could produce superlative poetry on the Taj Mahal, but I have never heard of anyone writing any poems on the pyramids.

But alas, the ordinance of indestructibility that the pharaohs had written did not last. The dynasties of the pharaohs crumbled; the Persians from a faraway land came to destroy Egypt; then came the Greeks and the Romans; finally the Egyptians accepted Islam as their religion and embarked on a new path. Muslims comprehended the difference between the body and the spirit. They understood that it was not necessary to mummify the body for an eternal life.

No point in finding faults in the pharaohs. All over the world, in almost every country, after reaching a peak of civilization people have said, 'We have reached the highest level. There is no need to progress anymore. Let us protect and keep intact whatever we have saved.' The result is the downfall.

There is no need for me to waste further words when Rabindranath has already composed a poem like 'Taj Mahal' on this subject.

19

People from around the world gather to see the Taj Mahal in the full moon.

The same is true of the pyramids.

The place was crawling with people. Possibly not even the fairs in this country get so crowded.

There were enough reasons for it too. In a hot country, unless it is winter, it is not possible to do sightseeing properly for long during the day. This is good in a way, particularly when there is no fine design work to see. The intricate latticework of the Taj is not visible in the moonlight but its overall symmetry, which becomes prominent at night, eludes us in the bright sun. Hence people go to see the Taj in the full moon. The pyramids do not have such subtle handiwork; and the desert all around makes the days painfully hot; hence except for the winters, few people go to see the pyramids during the day.

On the contrary, it is different in cold countries. In Cologne, I had walked past the cathedral on many moonlit nights, shivering, and never did I see a soul.

Sitting here I could hear a multitude of tongues of people from far and wide, the crumpling noise of the opening of sandwich wrappers and the popping sound of soda and lemonade bottles. A European cannot take three steps without carrying food with him. Be it the pyramid or the cemetery, after reaching the destination, he will say, 'Tom, please pass the basket. Dick, please pour tea from the flask,' and looking at his wife, 'Darling, you didn't forget to pack the apples I hope.' Meanwhile, Harry would have started playing the gramophone. And in case women were greater in number, you simply would not hear anything. In the cacophony of the hotchpotch of 'lovely', 'grand', 'sublime', one would be hard-pressed to figure out what was what.

Paul and Percy were back. I asked, 'What did you see, boys?' Then opening the notebook, I said to them, 'Tell me everything in detail, I'll note it all down; like a fool, I spent the entire time sitting here.'

Percy said in a pitiful voice, 'Please sir, no need to rub salt on the wound. Didn't see a thing. Couldn't even see the palms of my own hands in the dim light of the torch. With its help, we somehow reached a square room after traversing many tunnels. All empty. There wasn't even a broom in the corner. The guide said, "Enough, we need to go back now." Why did you not stop us from going in?'

I said, 'Would you have listened had I asked you not to go? The thought of not seeing the last bedchamber of the pharaoh would have stung all your life. This is like Delhi's *laddu*!'

He asked, 'What's that?'

I explained.*

Paul said, 'The guide was saying, the massive stones of the pyramids were dragged here from across the river. I didn't understand fully because of his English.'

I told him, 'Yes, that's correct. There was no stone this side of the Nile. So by cutting the stones on the other side, they transported them here on rafts. In those days, as they hadn't learnt the craft of wheel-making, they used to push the stones to move them forward. They made slippery channels with wood and bamboo. And we have heard that they used to pour barrels of oil to keep the path greasy. Wasn't it a marvel? Six such stones gathered together would be equal to a present-day train engine. We have seen when such an engine is derailed, how much effort, using cranes and pulleys, is required to bring it back on track. So how can one disbelieve the idea of pouring oil and butter?'

Then we discussed the idea of inventing the wheel. The way fire had shown men the path of civilization, the

---

* Delhi's *laddu*—the round sweetmeat of the Indian subcontinent—has attained such an aura that people from other parts are eager to eat it and often get disappointed. Hence the adage—*Delhi ka laddu: jo khaya woh pachtaya, no nahi khaya woh bhi pachtaya*—meaning Delhi's *laddu* is such that people are utterly disappointed if they have not eaten it and so are those who have tasted it.

wheel did the rest by facilitating its forward motion. I had heard that the wheel was invented in Mohenjo-daro and then it spread all over the world.

When we ride in a palanquin, we go back to the age when there were no wheels. Six men struggle to carry even a small girl; they rest every few moments and fan themselves with their towels. On the other hand, one rickshaw puller can quite easily pull two heavy bodies effortlessly with the benefit of wheels.

Abul Asfia said, 'They did not invent the wheel but they surpassed everyone with their precise handiwork. They could join tens of thousands of rocks, each weighing thousands of tonnes, with the precision of one thousandth of an inch. I doubt if jewellers and opticians today can show such precision. Jewellers work with an object of one inch or even half. They had to handle millions of inches.'

We asked, 'Why did they not then reflect such skills of precise craftsmanship in creating fine art and in aesthetics?'

Abul Asfia replied, 'That can be witnessed on the walls of their temples, in the stone statues.'

Alas, there was no way to see them now.

Percy by then had made a pillow by gathering sand and lying down with his head on it. From his birth, he had the God-gifted ability of monk-like detachment to theoretical discussions. I bowed my head to him.

Abul Asfia said, 'It's quite late at night. Let's go back to town.'

Paul was thinking deeply for a while. As we were walking to the car, he quipped, 'But I think this whole affair is a huge waste.' We all heard him quietly.

There was an elderly lady in our group. She said, 'No, Monsieur Paul. The pyramids have at least one quality. Standing in front of it when I compare its age, I feel I'm still a young girl.'

It was a worthwhile statement.

I said, 'Bravo.'

20

We look a certain way when we are awake but different when we sleep. The same rule applies for cities. A man who is awake can look sharp and brainy but the same man looks devoid of all intelligence when asleep. Laldighi* reverberates with cacophony in the middle of the day but the same place feels creepy at midnight. In our neighbourhood, the Park Circus tram depot area falls asleep at noon but the eateries there start a choral symphony in the evening.

In the field of aesthetics I do not differentiate between younger and older people. An eight-year-old enjoys reading the *Mahabharata*; an eighty-year-old gets the same satisfaction. On the other hand an eight-year-old can easily sing a *kirtan* song but an eighty-year-old learned man with no musical sense cannot even identify if it is a *kirtan* or *baul*. Meaning, the sense of aesthetics does not depend on age.

---

* Pond in the administrative quarters of Kolkata.

But there are smaller senses of aesthetics that depend on age. There is no point of smoking cigarettes at the age of eight; the joy of playing marbles on the street dries up at eighteen. Similarly, the city by night is not for children. Let me explain: I can send out an eight-year-old to call eight taxis during the day but I cannot send a ten-year-old to ten places at night.

But what to do with daredevil boys like Paul and Percy who were still up at two in the morning? Abul Asfia assured us that there were dance performances in Cairo where parents take their children to have fun.

It was decided to go for such a cabaret.

Open air. Open sky. Japanese lanterns with dim lights of various colours were floating all over us. Looking closely, one could spot flickering stars embedded in the sombre night sky.

Hundreds of small tables. To one side was the stage. There were no wings on either side but in the background hung what looked like the hood of a snake or a seashell. The seashell was corrugated to make it look like the ones found on beaches—it was beautiful. Was the green room located behind the backdrop or was it underground?

Suddenly the lights went off. I was wondering what was happening. I whispered in the ears of Paul and Percy, 'Hold onto your purses. Never know what can happen in this foreign land.'

No, after the lights came on, we saw a sphinx in front of the seashell. We had seen the stone sphinx next to the pyramids—but that was five hundred times bigger than this. The sphinx was the representation of the emperor of Egypt—the pharaoh. Only the head was of the pharaoh, the rest of the body looked like a lion to connote his might and power.

Six girls came out from behind the backdrop. Their bodies were covered from neck to heel with milky-white dresses like a long chemise. We had seen Egyptian women on the streets adorning such dresses but in different colours.

Slowly they started dancing, circling the sphinx. With slight steps. Like the silent walk of pigeons. Like the moon traversing the sky from one end to the other without trampling on the flowers of the stars.

They wore no ankle bells on their feet or bangles on their wrists. A simple soft tune played on the flute, the tambourine and drum repeating between the crescendos. Full of sadness and grief. As if the mother from this side of the Nile was calling her son on the other side. I had heard such calls many times. Whoever it was, I could hear my mother's voice.

The call changed. Now we heard a different voice—as if the mother was trying to wake up her son. At first there was the gentle request. Then it turned into a voice of hope and anticipation. The music was becoming louder. The steps were moving quicker. Not six but as if sixty girls were filling in the stage in gorgeous ripples with faster steps. There was not a single spot left to step on.

Like one who had figured out the mystery of magic by dreaming up a strange passage or hearing an unknown voice, I suddenly understood the meaning of the dance. These were no dance steps without meaning, no pointless hand gestures. The dancers were representatives of a new Egypt. They were trying to wake up the sphinx from its millennia-old slumber. After piercing the sleepy curtain, he would re-establish himself again in Egypt; after breaking through the fogs of foreign repression, the new form of the old sun would bring light to Heaven and the earth.

Was it an illusion? I saw that the sphinx had a smile on its face. Was it magic or was it the unworldly blessings of the Creator?

It turned dark again.

Like the way it falls on sleepy eyes, the final red light of the setting moon and the preamble of the first rays of day fell on my eyes.

All hail the land of Egypt.

21

Is there not an old saying in English—'Early to bed and early to rise...?'

And are there not a few material gains if one follows it?

There is more money in cities than in villages. There are schools and colleges on every street and there is no count of how many doctors and quacks toil and go hungry trying to keep the city folks alive forever. Possibly that is why folks in the cities do not care to go to bed and wake up early. On the contrary, village people are early risers. Possibly that was why the inhabitants of Cairo were still asleep—but not snoring.

Abul Asfia said, 'That's right, but Muslims have to wake up to offer their first prayer even before the first birds sing. Most of their big mosques and madrassas are in the neighbourhood of Azhar. Let's go there. Surely they have woken up.'

Good idea. But what was the point of coming this far to Cairo to see people offering early morning prayers? One can go to Zakaria Street in our beloved Kolkata.

No. This was apparently the old quarters of Cairo. But a lot younger than the pyramids—only one thousand years old, give or take a few years. For the whole world, the colourful images that the name of the romantic city of the Orient, Cairo, evokes, apparently could still be witnessed in this neighbourhood.

Trams had started plying. Compared to Kolkata trams, they were more rickety and as empty as schools and colleges on holidays.

Seeing the first tram, Abul Asfia quickly paid up the taxi drivers and sent them away. Everyone knew about this simple trick of saving money but who would know, in an alien land, which tram went where? In my own city, I often mix up trams and reach Maula Ali instead of Kalighat or, in a critical condition, I end up at Nimtala crematorium ghat, when I need to go to the Medical College. '*Hari bol*!'

Abul Asfia said, 'Allah is there, why worry?'

> Being your companion   In the blistering deserts
>   May I die by losing my way
> Leaving you behind   Going to the masjid
>   What will I get if I pray...

Still I was not that assured. Be it Allah or Hari, parking all Their important work, They were apparently supervising to make sure that the right tram came to the right spot for a bunch of vagabonds. I clearly lacked the deep belief that one needed to possess to have such confidence.

The street was becoming narrower—the way it is in every city when entering the congested old quarters from the new spacious parts of town.

The shops on both sides of the street were still shut. One or two coffee shops were about to open. A few Sudanese doorkeepers were counting their rosaries sitting on iron chairs on the pavement. There was a small gathering in front of the newspaper stalls, and the servants were hurrying, as they were late to reach the homes of their masters.

Streaks of light were gradually lighting up the liquid darkness. The white parting in the middle of black hair was becoming visible. There was a light daubing of vermillion on that. It was not as if the frolicking of nature was entirely comprehensible, but resting my head on the window of the tram in a semi-dazed state of trance, it seemed like I saw bits of all of those. It is difficult to express in words the experience of the half-asleep, half-dreamy and half-awake state. In images this can easily be captured. Possibly that is the reason why a painting of a sunrise always surpasses the description of the same in literature.

The most magnificent were the minarets of the mosques. People who have seen the Qutub Minar know the beauty of minarets. It looks like it does not belong to this dusty earth. As if it is the crown of some King of kings, it stands much taller than the people of the country in a bid to reach the blessings of God.

At least Qutub's feet had touched the earth. Many of these minarets were standing atop God's own room—the prayer hall of the mosque. But these knew they were getting close to Allah's abode, for I could clearly see they were becoming narrower and narrower towards the top as if in fear, much like how the stout, well-built boys in the class become meek and timid when facing the headmaster. But the heavens and the sun were giving them assurance. The sky was draping them in an azure sari—half of it already adorned, and the sun was trying to help them stand upright by sending the lasso of his light rays. Seeing this, Omar Khayyam had said:

> And lo! The Hunter of the East has caught
> The Sultan's turrets in a noose of light.
>
> (Fitzgerald)

Kanti Ghosh's English translation had quality but I have objections to this one. In his translation:

> The golden arrow of the Hunter God of the East
> Struck the high top of the palace's turret.

In reality, the rays of sunlight could strike the turrets like arrows or could capture it like a noose. There was not much difference. But mad poets use so many inexplicable metaphors that it is hard to keep count. In that case, it makes sense to stick close to the original while translating.

Egypt's mosques are world-famous and magnificent,

following close behind such nature's creations as the Nile and the man-made pyramids. A multitude of discerning visitors cross the seven seas to come to Cairo to see its mosques. The descendants of those who built the pyramids had constructed these too; but by then a little bit of Persian, Greek, Roman, and in more recent times, Arab blood had mixed with them. So they built the mosques differently. I had mentioned earlier that the pyramids, with their millions of tonnes of weight, were sitting, just like the kings who sat on the chest of their subjects, like juggernauts. People who had constructed the mosques were Muslims. They placed the King of kings, the Creator, over the rulers. Hence the minarets of the mosques went upwards to Heaven. Or one could say that they stood the way Muslims stand erect in front of God five times a day during their prayers. Hence the aesthetic of pyramids evoke fear while the mosques are full of poetic beauty.

I realized that Paul and Percy were devoid of any appreciation for such aesthetics. After reaching the middle of old Cairo, getting off the tram, we started basking in the unparalleled magnificence of a mosque; meanwhile they were behaving like boys who had to go to the Ganges in winter for a bath supervised by their mother. They were appreciating the views of the Ganges but were sceptical about taking a dip.

Percy was a bit of a straight talker. He shot his mouth whenever he felt like it, even if it was unpleasant. Paul's approach was slightly different. If Ashwatthama danced after drinking fake milk prepared by mixing flour and water, Percy would tell him in an instant that he was being cheated with a fake mixture that looked like milk; while Paul would wonder what the point of telling him the truth would be, since there was no harm done to anybody that he was joyous.

Percy said, 'Huh! What's the point! Pyramids? Yes, I understand that. They're colossal. Not a joking matter. Will I be able to build one like that? I agree that the mosque is magnificent but is it that difficult to build one like this?'

Paul, too, wasn't much awestruck seeing the mosque. I have mentioned that earlier. But he did not agree with this logic. He asked, 'Can you build one?'

'For sure.'

I said, 'I doubt that. With all the strange-looking machineries of today, is it not possible to build a pyramid? But the fine handiwork that you can see on the walls of the mosque, people don't have that skill anymore. And what if there are such people? It will only be a replica. If you dig a huge pond, nobody will say that it's a replica of some other pond. Even if you build a pyramid, it won't be a replica, as all pyramids look the same—only some are bigger, some are smaller. But if you copy *Hamlet* and send it to a monthly magazine, they won't publish it; they'll say it's a copy. Didn't like the analogy? Even if you can make an exact copy of the 'Mona Lisa', people will say it's fake though you paint like a master; they will say, ah; but nobody will say, wow.'

Paul asked, 'What the difference between ah and wow?'

I replied, 'We say "ah" when we're struck by a surprise like if it's a trickery of hands or things like that. Suppose someone is walking on a tightrope hundred feet above us or putting one's head inside the mouth of the lion—in short, all circus acts—we say "ah" to express our disbelief. Likewise for the pyramids, we say the same, "ah". But when we see the serene portraits of Amitabha Buddha or the face of Madonna steeped in motherly love, we say, "Wow! What relief! What beauty!" The degree of expression in "ah" is ultimately lesser than "wow" despite the fact that it may capture the most difficult or adventurous acts. However difficult it may be to climb Mount Everest, its worth is less than giving water to a thirsty person. As Percy said, he wouldn't be able to complete an arduous task like building the pyramids but that can't be the final benchmark. Shakespeare possibly couldn't dance on a tightrope but who will decide that such an act was superior to writing *Hamlet*? Actually, these are two different activities. There's the skill of engineering in pyramids, but the mosques contain artistic creation.'

Meanwhile, I noticed a student of Al-Azhar University, attired in an Egyptian gown, was approaching us from the mosque. He looked like an Indian.

22

Al-Azhar University is a whole millennium old. Even Oxford, Cambridge, Paris, Berlin are a few hundred years younger than it. Yet the names of all the learned people the world has known are products of these European universities. We do not get to hear about those who pass from Al-Azhar. Yes, I remember, the Gandhi of Egypt, Saad Zagloul Pasha was a student of Al-Azhar University. But why do not we know about anybody else?

Strange! When the Muslims occupied Spain, they established a university there modelled on Al-Azhar. Quite a few who were involved with the foundation of Paris University had studied in the Muslim university in Spain. And its early textbooks were translations from Arabic into Latin. Nobody talks about Al-Azhar these days, but they do talk about Paris University often.

But why was I surprised? Once upon a time the knowledge of India had spread all over the world. The Greeks learned a lot from us. In the following age, the Europeans learned the use of zero from us (possibly you know that the Roman numerals of I, II, X, XII, C or M had no zero) and as a result their mathematics progressed incredibly quickly. The Arabs translated Charaka and Sushruta,* and so many other texts. In the eleventh century Al-Biruni, the star intellectual of the court of Sultan Mahmud, the invader of India, wrote a tome on India† by learning Sanskrit. The entire Muslim world hailed India after reading that book. In a later era, when the book on the Upanishads, written in Farsi by Dara Shikoh, the elder brother of Emperor Aurangzeb, was translated in Latin, it created quite a stir in Europe. The greatest philosopher of the time, Schopenhauer, had said, 'This book will fill the last few days of my life with peace.' At that time, the poet of the world, Goethe, had said 'bravo, bravo' after reading the translation of *Shakuntala*.‡

Still, Europeans respect and value the old treasures of India and Al-Azhar. But nobody talks about people who study Sanskrit here or Arabic in Egypt. Why can they not produce something that will compel the readers to exclaim 'bravo, bravo'?

---

* Famous physicians of ancient India who penned one of the earliest pharmacopoeias.

† *Kitab-ul-Hind* is divided into eighty chapters and discusses religion, philosophy, society, science, astronomy etc of India.

‡ Sanskrit ballad *Abhijnana Shakuntalam* by Kalidasa, believed to be the poet laureate in the court of King Chandragupta Vikramaditya of Ujjain in the fourth and fifth century.

Alas, their creativity has dried up. Why did it dry up? The only reason being, after entering an age, they started thinking that everything has been done, nothing new needs to be produced; it was enough to live off the old heritage.

What was more dangerous was that they refused to learn from others. Their arrogance could leave anyone dumbfounded.

I asked the student of Al-Azhar, 'Are physics, chemistry, botany taught in your university?'

He asked back, 'What are those?'

I somehow explained with a lot of difficulty.

He said, what was the point of learning something that was not there in the Holy Scripture?

I said, 'So true. There is no way except for religion. But my brother, if you break your leg after falling down and the doctor says that you need to do an X-ray to pinpoint the fracture, then will the Holy Scripture give you the engineering needed to make the X-ray machine?'

I do not remember what he said. 'Religion will save all'—something of the sort. Meanwhile, Paul and Percy were getting fidgety. I mentioned earlier that theoretical discussions shut down Percy; I saw Paul too was becoming restless. After I stopped talking, I saw that they were bargaining with a shopkeeper.

What was the matter? All the bits and bobs that were found inside the pyramids were being sold there. I asked, 'Those must be very expensive; from where will we get money to pay for them and why has the Egyptian government allowed them to be sold in shops instead of displaying them in the museums?'

The shopkeeper said, 'The same things have been found in such great numbers from all those pyramids that the government has released them in the open market. The best of the lot, of course, has been preserved in the museums. Hence these are not that expensive.'

I was contemplating if I should buy something or not. At that moment, the student of Al-Azhar whispered in my ear, 'If it is so, what are they then doing in the factory behind the shop? Let's go and see it.'

I said, 'What's the point? Kashmiri shawls made in Germany, original and authentic khaddar made in Japan, and German medicines made in Kolkata, we have seen it all. What new things will we learn?'

I said to Paul and Percy, 'Copying from the boy sitting next to you in the exam hall and making such fake objects is the one and same.'

Paul replied, 'In the exam hall the teachers will box your ears if they catch you.'

I said, 'The government does the same here with them sometimes.'

I suddenly realized the language in which the student whispered in my ears was Bangla. I asked him instantly, 'Are you Bengali?'

He said, 'Yes.'

Then I heard he was from Bardhaman and had been here from the age of ten and had almost forgotten Bangla. He would go back to Bardhaman after four more years—so twelve years in total.

What will he do after going back? There will be no value to his knowledge of Arabic back home. But that was no surprise. If someone came back to Bardhaman after learning Sanskrit from Kashi, who will care? He will go hungry. This boy had the same fate. Nobody respected the knowledge of old scriptures.

But I saw that the boy was not worried at all. His religious father had sent him to learn religion. He would go back after completing his studies. Then things would take their own course.

Our team members were stopping in front of different shops. There was little shopping being done. There was more interest in seeing stuff as it did not cost a penny. We could have spent the whole day like this, but one of the group reminded us that we needed to catch the train to Port Said at eight. After we prompted Abul Asfia, he said, 'Let's go.' But there was no urgency in him.

Against our wishes, we boarded the tram. The student of Al-Azhar refused to leave my company after being able to talk in Bangla. He too accompanied us. The Arabic language was now the mantra of his life, but is it that easy to forget one's mother tongue?

The tram stopped with a jerk. What was the matter?

Another tram ahead of us had derailed while taking a turn and the rest were all queued up behind it. A few people were trying to put the tram back on track with an iron rod. There was more shouting than actual work. Old men and young boys in long robes were running around the tram. And so much advice, oozing out from inside as well as from outside. The madness that follows the doling out of sweets after Hari Kirtan in our land was no match for this hullaballoo.

As lookers-on we were relishing the chaos, when suddenly someone realized that we had a train to catch at eight. My body and mind were refusing to leave the drama. Because, by that time, two sides had been formed in an attempt to put the tram back on the track. People who had arrived from the depot were suggesting one strategy and the drivers and conductors of the trams on the street were waging a jihad against them. The matter had reached a point where both sides, armed with iron rods, were trying to take the debate on the supremacy of their own strategies forward by facing each other valiantly. The tram passengers and the lookers-on were standing behind both groups. And the street urchins attired in long robes were circling around them like whirlwinds and at times interrupting them by running through the crowd. Getting caught at times, they also received a slap or two.

All the signs were there of a top-rate fight brewing.

But alas, people have to leave the world with so many

unfinished good deeds. For example, I had vowed to thrash Nidhiram one day. But before I could fulfil the vow, I passed my matriculation exam. That rascal Nidhi remained in the school after he failed. How wrong, what injustice! I knew that Nidhi was empty-headed but so many heedless chickens passed matriculation. What harm would have happened if he passed too? I would have got the pleasure of giving him two blows on his back. I was disgusted with the whole world seeing such injustices all my life.

The same thing happened this day with the hurrying by our team. We did not have much time in hand. We had to take taxis.

There was a long queue—like the long curly tail of Hanuman in Bangla *jatras*—in front of the ticket counter. Some called it a U and some a W because sometimes the Q or the queue took various other shapes owing to a lack of space. But the train was leaving in five minutes. Abul Asfia joined the queue. I said to him, 'Surely we'll miss the train.' He said, 'You people enter the station.'

After checking which platform the train was to leave from, when we reached at the entrance of the platform, the ticket checker asked us in broken English,

'Where will you all go?'

'Port Said,' we said in a chorus.

'Then why aren't you boarding the train?'

Hearing that, a few of the group ran to the train desperately. Others remained stationary, failing to decide if they should go or stay. Three of us—Paul, Percy and I—did not move.

We said, 'We haven't been able to buy our tickets yet.'

The checker said, 'You can go.'

It seemed the young man was intelligent. Seeing our faces and appearances, he could figure out that we were not stowaways. There was no use stopping us when we were ready to pay our fares.

I was contemplating moving too. At that point I realized how decent of a man Paul was. He said to me, 'We'll not go without Abul Asfia.'

At that moment of crazy crisis, I remembered the epitome of justice, Yudhisthira, had refused to enter Heaven in a certain situation.

The huge station clock was right in front us. It was showing 7:59.

I could see through the collapsible gate that the train conductor was taking a slow heroic stride towards the train while looking at his pocket watch sporadically.

Egypt was a country of the Orient, a land of laid-back dispositions, a land of unpunctuality. From where did they finally learn the act of running trains on time? Again I began to despise the world. It was only a train; it travelled late almost every day. In the golden land of England, in whose praise the people of our land became all mush, even there, I heard that the train of a daily commuter ran late every day. The poor man wrote many petitions and one fine morning the train came exactly on time. Full of joy, the commuter congratulated the station master and the master said with a long face, 'It's yesterday's train, running exactly twenty-four hours late.'

If trains ran late in that land so close to our heart, why were the people, in this aristocratic Egypt, planning to start the train on the dot just to mock us?

I saw the guard approaching us slowly. After asking the ticket checker something and hearing his answer, he said to me, 'There's no time. Please get on the train.'

I was mesmerized by the courtesy of the man. Who were we? Why was there so much concern for us? He could clearly see that we were not rich American tourists that would cover him with gold. The trains of Egypt might have been built with iron machineries but the heart of the conductor was made of the blood of love.

I was desperately searching for words of gratitude in Arabic, Turkish and Farsi sentences so that I could express my thanks to him. English has only the poor 'Thanks', in French 'Merci', in German there is some donkey or danke. Would I be able to swim in the sea of gratitude for the conductor with those few words?

Still I daringly kept on saying, *'ana ushkurkum'* *'chok tashakkur edrong efendong'* *'khaile tashakkur,* *'midamhatan'*, *'qurban'* and many more. The gist was, 'India will forever, over generations remember the courtesy shown by your good sire but right now we are not being able to get into the iron cart because we are incapable of going to a foreign land while deserting our dear friend, our friend for life, Abul Asfia Noor Uddin Muhammad Abdul Karim Siddiqi.'

With that I profusely asked for his forgiveness in three languages—Arabic, Turkish and Farsi.

In my mind I was getting annoyed with Abul Asfia. Had the man no common sense? As the leader of the group had he no sense of responsibility? Possibly this was why India was still deprived of self-rule.

Suddenly Paul and Percy darted out. They had spotted Abul Asfia. And the strange thing was he was still very calmly talking to a railways staff, pointing at the big clock. He was surely trying to convince him of something silly. Certainly he was trying to tell him that their clock was running fast. Let it run fast; what would you gain by showing that to him? Would he grow a few strands of hair on his bald head? We were still nearly going to miss our train—

In the middle of his conversation, Paul and Percy grabbed him on both sides. Then they started running towards the train. I too was running for my life. The other team members who were waiting in front of the train uttered the victory cry. Abul Asfia was trying to free his hands. The international crowd in the station was staring at us. The policeman blew the whistle. Was it an attempted kidnapping?

It is turned on its head, man, turned on its head.
Where is the horse and in whose mouth is the rein?

Here two young boys were kidnapping a full-grown adult.

Whether the train left on time or late or if Abul Asfia's watch was right or the clock of the station, the answers to such minute questions were not resolved. The way the guard pushed us in with his practised hands, it was evident that he had plenty of experience of such situations.

Abul Asfia was still trying to convince Paul that his watch had won the first prize in the tests of chronometers in Switzerland. The Egyptians had no sense of time. We were gullible as well; we too had started running on hearing that the bird had snatched our ears—

23

Wow! What a beautiful land. Every few minutes, the train was crossing bridges over canals with the rolling sounds of gm, grm grrm. Then it would run to a rhythmic clickety-clack. Then again the gm, grm, grrm. Who knew that sounds of the train could be so sweet? I did not know what would have happened had we missed the train!

I said they were canals but some of them were so wide that I guessed they were tributaries of the Nile. The water was almost at the same level as their banks. Except for during monsoon months, the banks in our rivers stay much higher and the water level goes down. The banks get so high that the water becomes unusable. The farmers cannot drain it in winter for irrigation. From ancient times when the people of this land learned agriculture, their only river had created a mesh of thousands of canals and tributaries on both sides in such a way that it could never become too deep. Its water always remained full to the brim.

The fields were full of rice, wheat and cotton. Greenery

everywhere. Rows of date palm trees at intervals. Sometimes a single tree standing tall as if on guard.

And long boats were sailing on the river with their tall triangular sails. As there was hardly any rain in this country, they had no overhead cover. The boats were moving fast with the aid of the strong wind. They had no fear that the boat might capsize if the ropes of the sails broke. I guessed that sudden unruly winds did not destabilize the boats here.

Green fields, sails of different colours, the deepest of deep azure sky, the slow-flowing waters filled one's heart with serenity and total peace. Leaning my head on the train window, with half-closed eyes, I was thinking that people should surely travel by train to see this beauty. Had I lived in this country, I would have taken this train journey to an unknown destination every Saturday. Not for anything but just to look at the boats, the waters and the sky, day and night.

With the thoughts of the nights, I guessed that it would be a different kind of beauty in the moonlight. I did not get the opportunity to witness that this time.

At times, beyond the river, the boats and the date palm trees, I could see the three gigantic pyramids. We were so far yet it was as if they were running along with us with their faces on display. At that moment I realized how tall they were. I did not understand that fully when I was standing by them.

There was an aisle running down the middle of the train, like the trams in Kolkata. It was difficult to keep a count of how many peddlers of various items passed through the aisle. From oranges, bananas and breads, to notebooks, combs, socks, ropes, lottery coupons. It was difficult to believe there could be peddlers of such a variety of things. Except for an iron chest and a whole motorcar, there was nothing that was not hawked there.

In one corner I saw a maulana in long robes was giving a lecture animatedly, and a bunch of young boys, each wearing robes and a turban tied over a red fez, sat surrounding him. A few ordinary passengers too were listening to his lecture. Asking a fellow passenger, I gathered that he was a professor of Al-Azhar University. He was going to his home village and his close students were following him to continue their studies. The lecture continued all the way. Passengers of the train also got an opportunity to listen to him.

What a good system. It was an ideal combination of studying by staying at the teacher's home from days gone by and the modern system of going to colleges to attend classes. As the lessons were taking place in the middle of a third-class compartment, a few farmers also got the chance to enlighten themselves. Farmers in our country never get a drop of the ocean of knowledge imparted by professors.

The maulana was buying food from the vendors; he was feeding the students too. Everything was neatly taken care of.

All kinds of peddlers passed. Now came a strange fellow. There was a great smile across his face. Attired in a suit one size too big, soiled shirt, the somehow-done-up knot of the tie entering his collar, carrying a handful of handbills and pamphlets covered with colourful photos.

I could not say why he picked me out. Possibly he rightly guessed that I was the dumbest of the lot. It is well known that peddlers always target the most gullible ones.

Putting on another layer of smile over his already smiling face he asked me, 'Where are you going, sir?'

By travelling on a European ship, I had already acquired a bit of an English temperament. I was about to ask him what his interest was. But I remembered that Egypt was in the Orient; such questions are not considered bad manners or intrusions of any kind. I replied, 'Port Said.'

'Where after that?'

Suppressing the temper of the Mughals, I replied in a Bengali tone, 'Europe.'

'Oh, is that so? But Europe isn't going anywhere; meanwhile why don't you go and visit the country next to Egypt—Palestine?' I was dumbfounded. I had seen so many peddlers—some sold shoelaces for six pence and some gold watches for fifty pounds, but was it conceivable that an agent was on the train trying to sell an entire country? Yet I asked, in a bid to fully understand, 'Do you sell countries?'

Without replying to me and wearing another fresh coat

of smile on his face, he started looking for something from within the bunch of papers in his hand. Meanwhile the man next to me had given up his seat. Promptly taking his place, he fished out a faded pamphlet containing many colourful photos of Palestine. I saw, written in bold type font, 'Palestine, the Land of the Lord' and so on and so forth. Then he said, 'Sell countries? In a manner of speaking, yes, but not the way you've just suggested. That discussion can come later. But presently, see, I'm asking you to visit this beautiful country. The country where Lord Jesus Christ was born. You surely have heard the Lord's...'

I was annoyed to no end. What did these people think? That Indians did not know the name of Jesus? I blurted, 'The book of generations of Jesus Christ: the son of David, the son of Abraham. Abraham begat...' and so on quoting the psalms of the saints, I gave out Lord Jesus' full genealogy. The man was not one to be flustered easily. He kept on saying, 'So very right. See, this is the place where the Lord was born. In the stable of an inn. Mother Mary and her husband were coming to Egypt from Palestine through this route. It was evening when they reached the village of Bethlehem. Not getting a place in the inn, Mother Mary took shelter in the stable. See, this is the stable's photo. So many painters have done paintings of the stable over the ages. This is a photo of the village of Nazareth. Joseph worked there as a carpenter and Mother Mary used to go there to bring water. Here it is...'

I interrupted, 'Enough! Enough! But you can't understand my problem. If I decide to visit the Holy Land of Palestine of Lord Jesus after reaching Port Said, I shall have to buy another ticket to go to Europe after completing the trip. Who will pay for that? And let's assume I can somehow manage to pay for this pilgrimage. My pocket is still not deep enough to pay for the ticket again on the same liner.'

The agent was rolling with laughter. I was irritated. After controlling himself, he said, 'Why do you have to pay for the liner twice? Another ship of the liner you're using will arrive here, en route to Europe, in fifteen days. So you can board that one after completing your tour of Palestine.'

I stammered, 'Er, hm...but what if that liner has no empty cabins?'

The man had unlimited patience. To top it off, taking the saintly smile of forgiveness of Lord Buddha, he said, 'Why won't there be empty cabins? This is the off-season, slack period. So no rush of passengers. Isn't the ship you're travelling in half-full? The next one is almost empty.'

I remained silent for a while. Not because I was a thoughtful person. Actually, compared to others, it took me a long time to register things. The receiver set that Almighty Allah had put in my brain was of the most inferior quality. Their valves take a full three minutes to warm up. There are other troubles too. Three stations often get jumbled and create a cacophonous static sound. I often do not understand anything.

I suddenly had a brainwave. It was well known that the thickest of people too can raise some intelligent questions once or twice a year. So I asked, 'What's in it for you if I finally decide to go to Palestine? Will you grow hair on your bald head? What's your benefit?'

It seemed the man was now getting exasperated. I did not figure out why. Was it because it was a tough question or was it because I took a dig at his bald head? My brain, meanwhile, was panting at the labour of asking such an intelligent question.

He replied, 'My benefit? Not a lot. But there are crumbs. I will take you to Cook's office. You will buy your ticket to your first destination, Jerusalem—the capital of Palestine. You'll pay the fair fare, nothing extra. Cook will give me a commission—'

I asked, 'Why will Cook give you a commission?'

The man was now downbeat, witnessing the brightness of such 'intelligence' and said despairingly, 'The Palestinian government pays Cook Company to bring in tourists so that the government can raise some revenue. So they give them commissions and from that, Cook pays me a little. They can't go about in trains to look for prospective tourists. I do that job for them. Hence I make some money. Understood?'

I said promptly, to stop the man from hoodwinking

me, 'Yes, yes. I understand fully,' though I did not possess that much worldly intelligence to solve the complexities of commissions and subcommissions.

But I noticed he was looking at my valise. On it was written, in capital letters, ALI. The man asked, 'Is it your bag?'

I said, 'Yes.'

'Excellent. Then you're a Muslim. And Jerusalem is a Holy land for the Muslims too—its place is next to Mecca. Allah Almighty had brought Prophet Muhammad to Jerusalem from Mecca to show him Heaven. On that spot now stands the Masjid-al-Aqsa. A huge mosque with an intriguing construction. Just a few days ago your Nizam of Hyderabad spent ten lakh rupees to renovate it. Won't you go to see it?'

Then he said, 'You know what? Jerusalem is the confluence of three religions—Judaism, Christianity and Islam. You can kill three birds with one stone.'

I did not know if people won divine blessings through a pilgrimage. I never had to think about it in the past. But when I had seen Kashi of the Hindus and Rajgir of the Buddhists, why skirt away from these three? I never like the idea of favouring any particular religion. That is called communalism. When the Creator of the universe has come up with so many religions, surely all of them have some good in them. And my mother would be very happy if she heard that I had visited Baitul Muqaddas (the Holy

Jerusalem). Her father had reached Mecca but he could not see Baitul Muqaddas. I had heard that the best rosaries were sold there. She would be overjoyed if I could buy one for her. While praying seven times (normally Muslims pray five times a day but my mother offered prayers seven times), she will count the rosary I got for her and be very pleased with me.

***

Paul and Percy were heartbroken. Percy said, 'You are going to Palestine leaving us behind. Didn't you say that you'd show us many things while sailing on the Mediterranean, in Italy and Sicily, while passing through Corsica and Sardinia, Mount Vesuvius and so much else?'

But I was selfish, stony-hearted. I forgot my previous promises. Still I asked for their forgiveness with folded hands.

Paul said to Percy, 'Shut up, Percy. Sir loves to see places of religion. Why will he lose this chance?'

Still my heart felt heavy.

On the one side my friends and on the other my mother's rosary.

Why was the world full of such dilemmas?

Epilogue

The description of the visit to Palestine could have been a part of this book. But my apprehension is that younger readers will not like it without Paul and Percy's presence. That will make it a book for old people.

Authors dedicate their books to their friends after finishing them. I dedicate the unwritten travelogue of Palestine to my friends, Paul and Percy.

Acknowledgements

I sincerely thank Syed Musharraf and Syed Zaghlul Ali, sons of Syed Mujtaba Ali for giving me the permission to translate the book. I am especially grateful to Zaghlul Ali for passing on details of his father's fascinating life whenever we meet and talk over the phone.

The talented and budding poet Proiti Seal Acharya helped me with the translations of the poems and verses used by Ali in the text. Unless otherwise mentioned in the footnotes, the excellent translations of the poems have been done by her.

A project like this could not be finished without the help from the family. My son Aarjan diligently and painstakingly did the first copy editing. The 'bossy daughter' Prama breathed down my neck, compelling me to finish the translation when I put it on hold for a while, and became the first reader of the book.

I am deeply thankful to Sudeshna Shome Ghosh for doing a thorough editing of the manuscript.

Finally, my gratitude to Ravi Singh and Renuka Chatterjee of Speaking Tiger for taking this translation. Over the past eight years, since they published my translation of Mujtaba Ali's first book *In a Land Far from Home; A Bengali in Afghanistan*, there is no longer a publisher–author relationship—they have become friends.

www.ingramcontent.com/pod-product-compliance
Lightning Source LLC
LaVergne TN
LVHW041938070526
838199LV00051BA/2833